HEALING BEYOND TRAUMA

By Dr. Kristi B. Godwin, DPA, LMFT

Library of Congress Control Number: 2018905872
BeTheAuthorOfYourLifeBook@CreateSpace Independent
Publishing Platform, North Charleston, SC

First Printing, United States, 2018

ISBN-13: 978-1717574855

ISBN-10: 1717574858

<u>Dedication:</u>

To all the women who have been objectified, abused, tossed around, thrown away, neglected, and unloved. Know that total healing, peace, and freedom can be yours, if you will seek it with all of your heart. Break free of the chains of your past trauma and walk into a life you never imagined possible!

"For I will restore health unto you, and I will heal you of your wounds, says the Lord."

Jeremiah 30:17

Preface:

This book is intended to be a healing guide for those who have been affected by trauma or abuse. This book is not presenting a theoretical model, prescribing a set of beliefs, or intended as a guide for clinicians working with those who have experienced trauma. For those interested in the clinical after-effects of trauma, there is a DSM outline of PTSD as well as a description of the most research-proven effective treatment modalities for trauma included in the back of this book. For those seeking healing for themselves, there is a resource list of organizations and 24-hr crisis lines designed to help you in the back, as well. While I am a therapist, I am not presenting myself to be a leading expert in the area of trauma treatment, nor am I stating that the ideas discussed in this book are the only way to find healing. We are all on our own journeys, and we must find our own path. May love light your way!

"Although the world is full of suffering, it is also full of the overcoming of it."- Helen Keller

A Personal Note from the Author

Dear Reader,

Trauma is a topic very dear to my heart. I experienced trauma--physical, emotional, and spiritual trauma--from my earliest memories on. I lived it and had to learn ways to survive. I was blessed in that I didn't consciously recall the worst of my trauma until many years later, so I was able to live in oblivion much of the time. However, the trauma affected me on every level regardless. Once I became aware of it I was able to consciously process it and begin to heal from it. But, partly due to my own history, I was very close to many people who were traumatized, and it seemed as though I were a magnet of sorts that drew hurting and wounded people to me. I learned to listen, to help, and to heal very young. That is, everyone else! I am still learning how to heal myself!

I did go on to extensively study the human psyche, poring over texts at as young as 9 or 10 years old, and taking college courses in Psychology and Sociology as soon as I was allowed to (age 17). I sought out the tools that would make me an effective and compassionate therapist and still work diligently to hone my skill every day. I feel it is my purpose on this Earth to guide others to healing and wholeness, and I have been blessed in that I have been able to navigate some of these very dangerous and difficult waters myself before leading the way for others. The concepts I discuss in this book I have put into practice, not just in a clinical setting but in my own life. I have been able to attain a great level of peace and freedom myself from my own past wounds, and I believe these same tools have helped a number of others do the same. I would urge you to try them…what could it hurt? This is a journey only YOU can take, though, and it must be done in YOUR heart and YOUR mind and YOUR spirit, no one else can do those things for you. I pray at the end of this book you will think back to who you were when you began and be amazed at how far you have come!

I stand at the entrance to your freedom and I invite you to come. Don't stay chained to your past, weighted down by the pain caused you by others. Don't be continually tormented by your fear, your hurt, your memories. There is hope of walking forward completely FREE of all of that! I know, because I have done it.

Embrace your healing and share the tools with whomever you feel led!

Kristi Godwin

Acknowledgements

This book wouldn't be what it is without the encouragement and assistance of close friends who gave of their time and energy to help me edit and refine the message my heart wanted to present. My sincerest appreciation and gratitude to Heather, Andrew, and Jon for their suggestions and advice as I finalized this work. Thank you to Heather for formatting and spiritual advice, to Andrew for spiritual and grammatical advice, and to Jon for his clinical suggestions that helped make this a much stronger academic and clinical work. Thank you just doesn't seem like a strong enough expression, but THANK YOU from the bottom of my heart!! I also have to acknowledge Pastor Ronnie Hesters. Without his tutelage I would have never come to the understanding of the mind, body, spirit connection that I have. He helped me find the tools to walk into freedom, and now I am passing those tools on!

Table of Contents:

Chapter One: My Story.....

Part of my therapeutic orientation is that I do occasionally use strategic self-disclosure to help my clients feel heard, understood, and to give them hope. I believe therapists are designed to be carriers of hope and I do my best to fulfill this calling. In my experience, it does a great deal to engender hope when you encounter someone who has been through something similar to you and "made it out alive," so to speak. Of course, my story is my own and no two experiences are ever identical. Many times my clients have stories I cannot relate to and have no personal experience in. But sometimes, when I feel it is helpful for the client, I may share part of my story just to let them know there is hope beyond the place they are in at that moment. For the purpose of this book, considering that I have no way of knowing who may read it in search of hope and healing, I feel it is important for me to share a little bit of my own story. In fact, I've actually written an auto-biography (unpublished; my apologies to those of you who may be curious to read it) and it is twenty-five chapters long! So, for this purpose I will only include a few snippets of my experiences, just to give you an idea of what I had working against me when I began my journey. Because, let me tell you, if I can do it....SO CAN YOU!

So, I will start from the beginning. First of all, I experienced the wound of REJECTION from my primary parent at birth. For a long time I was unaware of just how big of an impact this had on me, but once my eyes opened I realized this was actually the biggest, most painful wound I had. And for those who can relate (Adopted? Raised by a family member? Foster care? Were your parents just emotionally detached? Or maybe even abusive?...All of those leave a sense of rejection that is very painful for a child, and even an adult), I promise you the other side of healing is AMAZING. Beyond that, I was adopted by a man who was an abusive alcoholic. And honestly, the more I examine my childhood from my adult-educated lens, I have trouble deciding if he was sociopathic, or maybe just narcissistic personality disordered. Either way, though, you can imagine my childhood was much less than idyllic. In fact, here is where I will share my first puzzle piece with you....This is a flashback of memory that stayed suppressed for thirty-five years, and when it resurfaced it caused quite a bit of re-evaluating to take place. So here is a piece of a memory that I blocked for over three decades, because facing it was just too unbearable. On this particular day, my adopted father was "babysitting" my brother and I while our mother worked. He had promised to take us on a wonderful picnic adventure, which ended up being not quite what he had led us to believe. Instead of a picnic, something much more gruesome and violent took place.

(WARNING: THIS ACCOUNT MAY TRIGGER SOME,

FEEL FREE TO SKIP IF NECESSARY):

I was trying so hard to be calm and believe this was just a dream and we would wake up and it would all be over. Then I remember being grabbed and restrained by them, and I could hear their laughter clearly. They were laughing at our futile attempts to fight them off and escape. I screamed and fought with all my might, and even screamed for my brother to run for help, but I saw he could not. The smell of stale cigarette smoke and beer-drenched body odor was almost nauseating, permeating my nostrils with every breath. As I struggled they jerked and twisted my right arm behind my back, and for a brief second, I was able to get my left arm loose. I stretched it out beseechingly toward my brother, the only person present who was innocent and "on my side." I screamed, "Get help!! Get help!!" Then the wind was knocked out of me as they threw my little body face down onto the ground and pinned me down with their knees and hands.

There was a throbbing ache in my cheek where it hit the ground on impact. The grit of the dirt mixed with small stones and broken bits of sticks dug into my skin as my cheek lay motionless, held there by the forceful pressure of his hand. I felt as if I were in some kind of dream...or rather, nightmare... because my mind just couldn't accept yet that this was really happening. In a glazed image, I could see my little brother struggling in the arms of our father some distance away. He was frantically trying to break loose, screaming and crying hysterically. I had already gone quiet and limp with the realization that no help was forthcoming. My voice was hoarse from screaming, though no one could know that because my mouth remained closed and silent. I had stopped struggling a few moments ago because it became clear that I was greatly overpowered, and my struggling only created anger and backlash in the form of physical pain. I didn't understand what was happening, but I knew that it was wrong to my very core. No child should be enduring this at the hands of her own family members, that I was sure of. A grave injustice was being done, one I was struggling to process and understand. What was going to happen to me? What were they doing? Was I destined to have only five years on this earth? My soul was overwhelmed with grief and pain so intense I could not comprehend or contain, then everything went quiet...

I will spare you the more graphic details, but suffice to say I was violently assaulted that day. The details reveal that it had cultic undertones and was a ceremonial ritual of sorts that I still to this day do not fully understand. Regardless, this event set in place a series of beliefs that I held onto for many years. Oftentimes our traumas do have beliefs, frequently UNTRUE beliefs, attached to them. One part of healing, I believe, is uncovering those false beliefs and confronting them with truth within ourselves. It is a process, to be sure, but one I strongly believe in.

In addition to the destructive familial patterns of an alcoholic and/or addicted family system, my family of origin included verbal and physical abuse, as well as very sophisticated psychological and emotional manipulation techniques. I won't go into details of those things, I only want you to know that they existed in my life and I do believe healing is possible from all of these. Another personal example of the various aspects of abuse and manipulation is one particular incident in which my father threatened to kill my younger brother to attain complete control over my mother, which is detailed below from my personal perspective as a young child:

Another time, my brother and I were asleep in bed, clueless to Daddy's drunkenness until we heard the sounds of loud, angry voices, and my mother's shrill, tear-filled, "No, don't!!!" As the voices got closer I tried to pretend to be asleep. Later I would learn my brother did the same. As my mother's screams reverberated in my ears, I peeked open one eye to see my father standing in the shadowed doorway to our room, holding a pistol in his hand. My mother was screaming "NO!" and frantically trying to grab the arm holding the gun. The gun was aimed toward my brother, still lying innocently in his bed. I prayed silently, "God, please don't let him wake up, please don't let him wake up." I knew if he sat up he would be dead. The bullets whistled past me and hit the wall just above where my brother lay. Many years would pass before I would really understand the events of that night, but as understanding came to me God revealed to me that in those moments we were safe in the shadow of His wings ("He will cover you with His feathers and under His wings you will find refuge; His faithfulness will be your shield and rampart. You will not fear the terror of night, nor the arrow (or bullet??) that flies by day....He will command His angels concerning you to guard you in all your ways." Psalm 91).

As part of the after-effects of growing up in this environment, my idea of what a "healthy" relationship looked like was a little skewed, to say the least. As a consequence, I later ended up in a very physically and emotionally abusive marriage (no surprise, right?). Here is a description of one of the instances in that relationship where I had to seek help from law enforcement:

Upon his entrance I could sense a barely concealed violence. Instinctively, I was very quiet and subdued, not sure what was coming next. When he asked us to accompany him somewhere, I went without protest, eager to comply and keep him happy. On the drive, though, he seemed intent on criticizing me in every way he could. He was very angry at me, although I could not understand what I had done wrong. He was driving erratically, screaming as he drove. I was afraid we were in danger, so I asked him to let us (me and our son) out, saying we could just walk home. He refused. He slammed my face into the passenger car window, causing my nose to bleed profusely. Later, I realized he actually broke my nose with that action, but at the time I was too focused on surviving to think that far. He began punching me in the stomach with his right arm, driving with his left all the while. I tried to get my cell phone to call for help, but he snatched it out and slammed it on the dash until it broke. I quickly climbed to the back seat while he was distracted and considered if I could get my son (only two at the time) out of the car while it was still going. I gauged the speed and surrounding environment, but was afraid that we were going too fast for us to be able to survive the fall. I sat, tensed and ready to run as soon as the car slowed down enough. When we arrived home, I immediately took my son out of his seat and ran as if our lives depended on it, screaming for help all the way. Half-way down the drive way, my husband seemed to come to his senses and calmly, coaxingly, offered to let me take my car. I naively believed him, and walked back toward him. As soon as I was close to him, he reached out and snatched our son out of my arms. He then threw my car keys out as far as he could and jumped in his truck and raced off. Hysterical and terrified for my son's safety, I found my keys as quickly as I could and drove toward the local police station. I was more worried for my son than I was about my own condition, but the police insisted I be checked out by EMTs (I was bruised, bloody, and my clothes were ripped and bloodied, so I suppose in retrospect that was reasonable of them).

After I escaped that relationship with my son I suffered PTSD (Post-Traumatic Stress Disorder) symptoms for several years. It was only through therapy and my own active pursuit of healing that I now walk free of the damage done. I feel it is important for you to understand that I was first rejected by a biological parent, then physically, sexually, and emotionally abused as a child by a parent (who was most likely personality disordered), as a teen I was raped, and later as an adult I was in more than one abusive relationship. I have been personally abused despite my education, in spite of my strong belief that violence is wrong, in spite of my efforts to understand and break all the cycles I was born into. But still I hold the belief and hope that I, and anyone else, can be completely free of these things, can live a happy and peaceful life, and can have healthy relationships. I believe it takes a deliberate choice to pursue these things and a willingness to do the work, however difficult it may be. It is my hope that the coming chapters will help you find your freedom, just as they have helped me find mine.

Chapter Two: The Scars Left Behind.....

One reason most of us live the rest of our lives carrying our battle wounds and being crippled by the various metaphorical scars of the wars we have fought to survive is that the wounds left by trauma are often largely invisible. Because they go unseen they go unaddressed, unattended, and unhealed. Many of you may not realize they exist, but even if you "feel" them in some ways, society would have us ignore them or pretend they aren't there. So, those of us who have them limp along as best we can, stuck perpetually in survival mode. I know this all too well. I was stuck in survival mode, or what we therapists like to term "fight-or-flight" mode, for forty years. I am not kidding—boy, do I wish I were! Literally, for four decades of my life I existed always in this state of agitation, hyperarousal, with one foot out the door in case I needed to run. That is no way to live, let me tell you! The problem was that this was the only normal I had ever known, so I was oblivious to the fact that I was stuck there.

I used to think trauma only referred to a catastrophic event, like being on the receiving end of a bomb and having some limbs blown off, or falling out of a four-story window. I never considered that trauma was anything I had ever experienced. I didn't realize that a trauma is any event or experience (including witnessing of one) that overwhelms your ability to cope in that moment. That is a pretty broad definition, and can mean different things to different people. In fact, traumas can be categorized as "Big T" and "little t" events. "Big T" traumas include things such as: natural disasters, rape, sexual attack, physical or sexual abuse, a life-threatening car accident, combat, and being robbed or beaten. "Little t" traumas include things like: non-life-threatening car accidents, divorce, infidelity in relationships, unexpected job loss, betrayal by someone close, financial or legal difficulty, and interpersonal conflict. Most people encounter a variety of "little t" traumas in their lifetime, but if a person encounters an exorbitant amount of "little t" traumas in conjunction with one or more "Big T" traumas, they may develop what's known as C-PTSD (Complex-PTSD). Those "little" traumas have a bigger impact than they get credit for.

As these traumas accumulate in your journey, they begin to take a toll on you, emotionally and physically. These "wounds" often show up in various ways. Here are some of the "hints" my body gave me, which I sometimes took to the medical professionals in my life, and also occasionally to the mental health professionals, as well: chronic headaches, chronic migraines, constant muscle tension (which led to back pain, neck "crinks", and other forms of chronic pain), difficulty sleeping, trouble breathing, adrenal fatigue, suppressed immune system, and stomach ulcers, just to name a few. The problem is our society is so divided that no one makes the whole-body connection. We are triune beings: mind, body, and spirit—those aspects of who we are often bleed into and intermingle with the others. The doctors address the physical (and usually ONLY the physical symptoms), the therapists address the mental/emotional (and usually ONLY the mental/emotional symptoms), and the pastors/ministers address the spiritual (and usually ONLY the spiritual symptoms). It is really up to US to be our own advocate and look at the whole picture of who we are to find out where the imbalance is, and what the true root of the issue is in order to attack it and heal it from the root up. That is the only way that works, I promise. If the root is ignored then the symptoms will keep appearing somewhere—defective fruit, diseased leaves, dying branches, or issues with the trunk (excuse the tree metaphor). You get the idea—if the disease is in the part of us that feeds the rest of us (the ROOT), then it will keep making us sick in some way or another until we find and address the actual primary disease.

See the illustration of this concept on the following page for a better understanding of this theoretical idea.

"The root of all health is in the brain. The trunk of it is in emotion. The branches and leaves are the body. The flower of health blooms when all parts work together."

-Kurdish saying

Illustration of Tree Metaphor

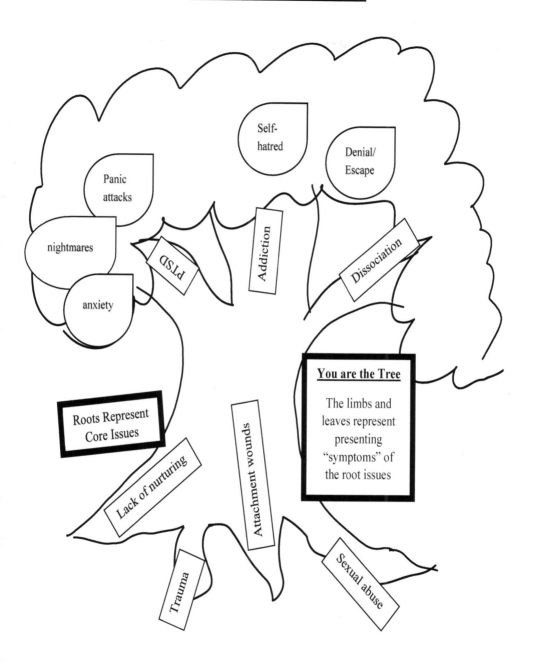

Now that I have covered the basic idea I will be operating from here, I want to discuss in a little more detail how trauma radically changes you. To do this I will pull from the work of one of the most respected Academics in this field, Boston-based Dutch psychiatrist and pioneering PTSD researcher, Bessel van der Kolk. His book "The Body Keeps the Score: Brain, Mind, and Body in the Healing of Trauma," has revolutionized the way most of us approach and understand trauma. His theory is that our bodies do keep score and that the memory of our traumas are "…encoded in the viscera, in heartbreaking and gut-wrenching emotions, in autoimmune disorders, and skeletal/muscular problems, and if mind/brain/visceral communication is the royal road to emotion regulation, this demands a radical shift in therapeutic [and medical] assumptions (van der Kolk, 2014, p.88)."

Van der Kolk observes, studies, and addresses what he terms "the extreme disconnection from the body that so many people with histories of trauma and neglect experience" using three main areas: neuroscience, which deals with how mental processes function within the brain; developmental psychopathology, concerned with how painful experiences impact the development of mind and brain; and interpersonal neurobiology, which examines how our own behavior affects the psychoemotional and neurobiological states of those closest to us (2014, p. 89). Basically, survivors of trauma tend to disconnect in ways that promote their functionality and survival, but this creates difficulties. As I have learned in this journey we call life, if I numb or disconnect myself from pain or sadness, I simultaneously numb my ability to experience love and joy. We cannot experience the "good" without also experiencing the "bad." Our attempts to block pain and discomfort only lead to us existing in a state of perpetual numbness, which, in my opinion, is something less than truly living life. Van der Kolk refers to this conundrum as the greatest challenge for survivors:

> *"In response to the trauma itself, and in coping with the dread that persisted long afterward, these patients had learned to shut down the brain areas that transmit visceral feelings and emotions that accompany and define terror. Yet in everyday life, those same brain areas are responsible for registering the entire range of emotions and sensations that form the foundation of our self-awareness, our sense of who we are." (Bessel van der Kolk, 2014, p.92).*

Numbing is what comes naturally to victims of trauma, however. It is what allows us to go on and survive. In doing our best to appear "okay" and "normal," we become experts in self-numbing. We seek numbing and distracting from any outside source we can find. Van der Kolk notes that many survivors become addicted to exercise, work, or become anorexic or obese (2014). Half of trauma survivors use drugs and alcohol to numb their intolerable emotions and thoughts (van der Kolk 2014). This becomes a problem when the numbness prevents experiencing a full range of emotions, and interferes with our ability to have healthy, fulfilling relationships.

Van der Kolk found that this ability to allow oneself to feel emotion was strongly and directly tied to one's ability to feel safe in any given environment or relationship. He wrote,

> *"Being able to feel safe with other people is probably the single most important aspect of mental health; safe connections are fundamental to meaningful and satisfying lives."* (van der Kolk, 2014, p.79).

This idea correlates with Brené Brown's research on vulnerability. Dr. Brown promotes the idea that vulnerability is directly tied to the ability to connect with others. We guard ourselves against betrayal and hurt, but in doing so we prevent ourselves from connecting at all. Another thing we do to "guard" ourselves is to numb our pain. We don't want to feel discomfort, so we disconnect from the discomfort. The problem with that, as Brown says, is that we cannot selectively numb emotions (2012). When we numb the painful emotions, we also numb the positive emotions. In essence, we numb our joy and pleasure simultaneously with our pain. We can't feel joy, or love, or pain. We just don't feel anything. What is the point of life if we are walking through it apathetic and oblivious to the pleasures of it? We must choose to be brave and face the world head on, whatever may come. Pain, love, joy….we have to FEEL whatever comes our way. We have to choose to be transparent, real, and vulnerable in order to have true, valuable relationships with others and fully live our lives. Vulnerability takes courage, but it is the only way to be true to ourselves and to also have healthy, loving relationships. A challenge for survivors of abuse, certainly, since "the promise of closeness often evokes fear of getting hurt, betrayed, and abandoned," (van der Kolk 2014, p. 215). But it is not insurmountable. Healing starts with a decision to live a vulnerable life before others. Start there, one step at a time. You will be glad you did!

According to van der Kolk, being connected into a good support network is the most powerful protection against traumatization and for healing (2014). "Traumatized human beings recover in the context of relationships with families, loved ones, AA meetings, veterans' organizations, religious communities, or professional therapists," (van der Kolk 2014, p. 212). Vital aspects of these connections are physical and emotional safety, and freedom from shame and judgement. Van der Kolk's research demonstrates the necessity of loving connections for healing. In order to change and heal, people need to experience the opposite of what they were traumatized by (van der Kolk 2014). Instead of fear, neglect, rejection, and pain, they need to be viscerally immersed in safety, connection, acceptance, and happiness.

"Wounds are what break open the soul to plant the seeds of a deeper growth," but those wounds will fester if left undressed (Voskamp 2016, p. 26). Wounds let in wisdom, but wisdom alone will not heal them. In other words, pain needs love to heal. Traumatic wounds need a loving connection to soothe them into oblivion, because "somehow love can lodge light into wounds," (Voskamp 2016, p. 26). Love shines light into the darkness and brings all things hidden into sight. Only love, perhaps, can heal these wounds.

Love heals all wounds

REJECTION

If you have experienced rejection by a parent, a friend, a loved one, a significant other, or even a stranger, you may still be carrying around that hurt. If so, try saying aloud the following:

(NAME OF PERSON WHO REJECTED YOU) , you hurt me deeply when you rejected me. But I realize NOW that there is nothing wrong with me that caused this...there is something wrong with you. I choose now to accept this and to forgive you. I forgive you for rejecting me and hurting me. I accept that I am worthy of being loved, I am loveable, and I will move forward knowing this. From now on I will allow myself to be loved the way I deserve to be. I won't let you hurt me anymore.

I forgive you and I am letting what you did to me go. I release you to my Higher Power. May you find healing for your brokenness as I am for mine. I will not carry this pain or this hurt or the damage you did to me around with me anymore. I leave it here, now. May you be blessed.

Chapter Three:
Spiritual Roots of Disease....

A principle I have come to understand more fully and believe very strongly is that we are not just a physical being, but we are TRIUNE. By this I mean that we are three parts in one whole: we are comprised of a physical body, an intellectual mind, and a spiritual being. Only when we address all three aspects of who we are can we find true wholeness and healing. "The part can never be well unless the whole is well," (Plato).

To my delight, the medical and scientific communities are beginning to recognize and acknowledge that this is, in fact, true.

Research is beginning to show evidence of the strong and irrefutable connection between the body, the mind, and the spirt in the human species.

There are consequences on multiple levels when we hold onto anger, hatred, bitterness, resentment, and unforgiveness. Medical science now classifies unforgiveness as a "disease" (Johnson 2015). Doctors are now aware of the reality that refusing to forgive others makes people sick and keeps them sick. Extensive work is published in this area by Dr. Steven Standiford, chief of surgery at the Cancer Treatment Centers of America. You are more than welcome to do some research of your own, you will find an abundance of information out there linking disease and unforgiveness. This is because when we hold onto things in our emotional hearts and spirits, our spirit becomes sick. Unforgiveness is like poison to our spirit, and that poison seeps out into our minds and bodies, as well. Our spirits, minds, and bodies are so connected they are essentially ONE and one area always affects the others.

Dr. Michael Barry is quoted as saying, "Harboring these negative emotions, this anger and hatred, creates a state of chronic anxiety. Chronic anxiety very predictably produces excess adrenaline and cortisol, which deplete the production of natural killer cells, which is your body's foot soldier in the fight against cancer," (2010, p. 84). With this realization at the forefront, medical professionals are now using "forgiveness therapy" to treat various diseases, including cancer. Dr. Michael Barry has conducted research in this area which reveals that of cancer patients that participated, 61% have forgiveness issues, more than half of which are severe forgiveness issues (2010).

"Failing to forgive, or unforgiveness, is the practice of engaging in ruminative thoughts of anger, vengeance, hate, and resentment that have unproductive outcomes for the ruminator, such as increased anxiety, depression, elevated blood pressure, vascular resistance, decreased immune response, and worse outcomes in coronary artery disease. Practicing forgiveness enables the transgressed individual to reduce their engagement in rumination thus reducing their experience of anger, resentment, and hate. Forgiveness, then, is a pathway to psychological well-being and health outcomes," (Norman 2016, p. 122).

If you think about how we deal with hurt, anger, and unforgiveness in our lives, it definitely makes sense that this would be an issue. You may replay the hurts in your mind for days, months, or even years after the event(s) occurred. In doing this you repeatedly re-experience the same anger, hurt, sadness, and frustration you experienced when the event first happened. This perpetual state prevents your heart from resting and you begin to suffer various physical and emotional issues as a result.

Many long-term illnesses are an outcome of unforgiveness, bitterness, and emotional stress. Chronic anger or fear lead to constant muscle tension which results over time in spasms, back pain, migraine headaches, fibromyalgia, and other forms of chronic pain (van der Kolk 2014). Anger is also known to lead to depression, anxiety, hypertension, and heart disease. Nearly 20 years of research now link forgiveness with better psychological and physical health (Barry 2010). These studies showed significant decreases in depression, anxiety, post-traumatic stress, self-esteem, and coping skills among people who practiced forgiveness in their lives. Karen Swartz, a psychiatrist from Johns Hopkins, also points out that forgiving reduces your risk of heart attack, improves your cholesterol levels as well as your sleep, reduces pain, blood pressure, anxiety levels, depression, and stress. "There is an enormous physical burden to being hurt and disappointed," states Karen Swartz, M.D. (director of the Mood Disorders Adult Consultation Clinic at the Johns Hopkins Hospital). The aftereffects of this keep you in fight-or-flight mode which affects your heart rate, blood pressure, and immune response over time. This increases your risks of heart disease, diabetes, depression, and other conditions, but these changes can all be reversed by one simple act: FORGIVING.

When I educated myself on all of this, I reduced it down to one simple question. For me, to continue to hold onto old hurt, anger, resentment, and unforgiveness was to slowly poison myself to death, to sit idly by while my body deteriorated because of it. To forgive meant I could LIVE. It really all boils down to this one question, "Do you want to live, or do you want to die??" You decide. If you put this decision off and in the meantime are still holding on to unforgiveness, then let me point out that your lack of choosing is in fact a choice. You are choosing DEATH by inaction.

Your life is in your hands. What will you do with it?

"Health is a large word. It embraces not the body only, but the mind and spirit as well; …and not today's pain or pleasure alone, but the whole being and outlook of a man."

-James H. West

"Holding on to resentment is like drinking poison and expecting the other person to die."

-Nelson Mandela

Chapter Four: Forgiving Your Abuser(s)....

I know what you're thinking, "How could I possibly forgive them?? What they did was UNFORGIVEABLE!" Sometimes it feels as if we, the "victims," are having to do all the work, while the perpetrators of our abuse get to waltz through life carefree without consequence. It seems that way, I know, but trust me...it's an ILLUSION. This is yet another of those false beliefs we often take on after trauma which comprises most of the bars of the prison we live the rest of our lives in. UNLESS we can find the truth that is the key that unlocks that prison. If there is ONE truth that is the master key to freedom for you, let me tell you....FORGIVENESS is it!!

There is no easy way around it. You cannot escape it. The only way to freedom is through it!

But let me clarify a few things. One thing I realized in my own journey to forgiveness was that some part of me, deep inside, believed that I was in part responsible, or even in control maybe, of making sure my abuser(s) got the punishment they deserved. And if I "let it go," or forgave them, I was letting them off scot-free, without any punishment. I held on to that anger, that trauma, that hurt, for dear life! Surely, they deserved to pay for what they did to me! I believed forgiving them meant me psshawwing their wrong, in essence saying "Oh, it's OKAY! No big deal! Just go on as if it never happened, I'm FINE!" And that would be a lie. I could not go along with that lie, not even in pretense. I wasn't fine. I would never be "fine" again. I was irrevocably altered by the events I suffered at their hands. And nothing would ever change that. So how could I forgive them???

Then a really wise lady I sought counsel from on occasion said to me one day, "*Holding on to unforgiveness, and bitterness, is like drinking poison and waiting for someone else to die.*" WHOA!!

That drove into my heart like a knife! What that said to me is that instead of punishing my abuser by withholding my forgiveness, I was actually punishing myself! Hadn't I suffered enough already? I had to really give that some thought. So, I started doing some research. What I found was astounding. Medical science has researched and found a connection between unforgiveness, bitterness, and anger with heart disease, heart attack, stroke, and even cancer. Medical doctors are seeing that there is a very real connection between the spiritual heart or spirit, and the physical heart and body. So, if holding on to unforgiveness could actually cause me to have a heart attack, or a cancerous tumor to grow, and KILL ME, then I was in essence KILLING MYSELF by holding on to my hurt. A righteous anger rose up in me at the very thought of that. I was the victim! I was abused and traumatized, through no fault of my own, and I might die because of it?? That's when I started developing the motivation to actually forgive and let go. If forgiving meant that my abuser(s) no longer had power over me, and could no longer hurt me every time I remembered the abuse, and that I, too, could go on with my life, carefree, almost as if it had never happened....then okay, I'm in! Let the forgiving commence!

If only it were that simple....Simple it is, easy it is not. It is simple, in that it really is a choice you can make for yourself (not for THEM, but for YOU). You can choose to forgive, and in doing so unlock the prison you were placed in by your abuse and trauma. Sometimes that is much harder than it seems. We just want to hold on to those deep, deep wounds with all we have. We want justice to be served and we think we can somehow control that. In holding on, though, you are not forgiving. Just like you can choose to forgive, you can also choose to stay imprisoned. But why would you?? If you know you have freedom just one step away, why would you refuse to take that step?? But people do just that, all the time. What will you choose to do? For me it became a very black and white decision. I broke it down to life or death. I could choose to hold on to the unforgiveness, but in doing so I would be choosing my own death. Yes, sure, maybe I could live a few more years, but I would be miserable, lonely, angry, and bitter, isolated in a prison of my own making. What kind of a life is that?? OR, I could choose to

FORGIVE, and in doing so I would be choosing to walk out of the prison into a life of freedom in which I could potentially experience peace, love, joy, and happiness like I had never known. And THAT would be truly living!! So, what to choose...life or death?? I chose life!!! And I have not, not even for one millisecond, ever regretted that choice. Instead I chide myself for putting it off and cheating myself out of the peace and happiness I now WALK IN DAILY for so long!

So how do you do this? You just do it! Everyone will develop their own individual process that works best for them, but I'll share my process with you and you are more than welcome to try it for yourself. I encourage you to do this your own way, though. As long as you don't skip important steps or gloss over it and not actually forgive! Trust me, I've done that, too!! I was 33 the first time I really forgave someone. I had said I had forgiven them many times before that, and even had forgiven to some degree. But at 33 I realized I was still holding on, at least a little bit on some levels, to every single hurt I'd ever experienced. And if you're holding on, that means you haven't truly forgiven yet.

So, I sat down and methodically went back through my life and thought of every single hurt I had ever experienced. And it was a lot!! I had a notebook, and I filled up a few pages...just with the names of the people who had hurt me (not what they had done). Rows and rows of names. People who had rejected me, mocked me, abused me, betrayed me, lied to me, stolen from me, abandoned me.....you get the idea. ANY hurt at all, I wrote the name down on my list. And then I started going down the list, forgiving one by one.

I used a three-step process to forgive; I'll expound a bit more on those steps in another chapter. For the purpose of forgiving, though, forgiveness is only step one. The second step is releasing them to your Higher Power, God as you understand Him/Her, and letting go of the hurt, anger, and bitterness. The final step is a "test-step"....it is to ask your Higher Power to bless him or her. If you can truly, sincerely from your heart, ask for blessings for your abuser, then you have forgiven and released them.

1. FORGIVE

2. RELEASE/LET GO

3. BLESS/WISH WELL

Once you have completed this step you should be able to think of the person who hurt you, the things they did that hurt you, and feel no real pain or anger at all any longer. It should be an objective memory without strong emotion attached. If you have not achieved that level of peace with it yet, then go back to step one and go through the process again. It may take a few tries to fully forgive. That is okay. What is not okay is giving up and continuing to hold on to the toxic unforgiveness, and choosing to stay in your prison. Fight for your freedom! You deserve it!

If you do find it difficult to forgive, a method often recommended is to "pray for your enemies" daily until you are able to forgive. If prayer is not something you practice, consider starting a new habit. Research shows that prayer is a protectant against depression and that it does aid in healing (Miller 2013). Dr. Lisa Miller, professor and director of Clinical Psychology at Columbia University conducted a study that shows that people who valued their religion and prayed regularly had thicker cortices in the brain which indicated a lower chance of depression (2013). Another study, conducted by Dr. William Harris of the Mid America Heart Institute in Kansas City, MO, demonstrated that patients who were prayed for over the course of one year had eleven percent fewer heart attacks and strokes than patients who had not been prayed for (1999). So prayer appears to have value and effectiveness even in the scientific and medical communities. Why not give it a try?

<u>Below, you will find several different forgiveness models to use:</u>

<u>Sample prayer of forgiveness:</u>

Dear Heavenly Father,

    I forgive _____ *for hurting me by* _____. *I forgive him/her and ask You to forgive him/her, too. I release them into Your hands, for You to do as You see fit. I let go of all the pain, anger, bitterness, and resentment I have toward them about this. I ask Your forgiveness for holding on to this hurt for so long. I also ask You to bless them, to bring them into right relationship with You, and to give them a good life.*

In Jesus' Name,

Amen.

Forgiveness Worksheet:

People I need to forgive: | Offense they committed:

1 _____ | _____

2 _____ | _____

3 _____ | _____

4 _____ | _____

5 _____ | _____

6 _____ | _____

7 _____ | _____

8 _____ | _____

9 _____ | _____

10 _____ | _____

11 _____ | _____

12 _____ | _____

13 _____ | _____

14 _____ | _____

15 _____ | _____

16 _____ | _____

17 _____ | _____

18 _____ | _____

19 _____ | _____

20 _____ | _____

Forgiveness Worksheet:

People I need to forgive:	Offense they committed:
21	
22	
23	
24	
25	
26	
27	
28	
29	
30	
31	
32	
33	
34	
35	
36	
37	
38	
39	
40	

Enright Forgiveness Process Model (Enright 2001)

PRELIMINARIES

Who hurt you?

How deeply were you hurt?

On what specific incident will you focus? '

What were the circumstances at the time?

Was it morning or afternoon? Cloudy or sunny?

What was said? How did you respond?

PHASE I—UNCOVERING YOUR ANGER How have you avoided dealing with anger? Have you faced your anger? Are you afraid to expose your shame or guilt? Has your anger affected your health? Have you been obsessed about the injury or the offender? Do you compare your situation with that of the offender? Has the injury caused a permanent change in your life? Has the injury changed your worldview?

PHASE 2—DECIDING TO FORGIVE Decide that what you have been doing hasn't worked. Be willing to begin the forgiveness process. Decide to forgive.

PHASE 3—WORKING ON FORGIVENESS Work toward understanding. Work toward compassion. Accept the pain. Give the offender a gift.

PHASE 4—DISCOVERY AND RELEASE FROM EMOTIONAL PRISON Discover the meaning of suffering. Discover your need for forgiveness. Discover that you are not alone. Discover the purpose of your life. Discover the freedom of forgiveness. (Enright 2001)

Nine Steps to Forgiveness

1. Know exactly how you feel about what happened and be able to articulate what about the situation is not OK. Then, tell a couple of trusted people about your experience.

2. Make a commitment to yourself to feel better. Forgiveness is for you and no one else.

3. Forgiveness does not necessarily mean reconciling with the person who upset you or condoning the action. In forgiveness you seek the peace and understanding that come from blaming people less after they offend you and taking those offenses less personally.

4. Get the right perspective on what is happening. Recognize that your primary distress is coming from the hurt feelings, thoughts, and physical upset you are suffering now, not from what offended you or hurt you two minutes—or 10 years— ago.

5. At the moment you feel upset, practice stress management to soothe your body's fight or flight response.

6. Give up expecting things from your life or from other people that they do not choose to give you. Remind yourself that you can hope for health, love, friendship, and prosperity, and work hard to get them. However, these are "unenforceable rules:" You will suffer when you demand that these things occur, since you do not have the power to make them happen.

7. Put your energy into looking for another way to get your positive goals met than through the experience that has hurt you.

8. Remember that a life well lived is your best revenge. Instead of focusing on your wounded feelings, and thereby giving power over you to the person who caused you pain, learn to look for the love, beauty, and kindness around you. Put more energy into appreciating what you have rather than attending to what you do not have.

9. Amend the way you look at your past so you remind yourself of your heroic choice to forgive. (Greater Good, 2004)

Chapter Five: Letting Your Pain GO.....

So, what happens to the people who wronged us? Do they get off "scot-free," as we so fear? The reality is that we have ZERO control over their punishment. Within the confines of the law, there is limited recourse to bring justice to our situations. Sometimes there is no recourse at all. That is the sad reality. But the good news is that we do not have to take matters into our own hands, nor do we have to trust the legal system to always protect us (in many cases it cannot). There are universal principles at play here which will handle the matter for us, without us doing a thing. It is our responsibility, though, to release our judgement to something greater than ourselves. One principle at play here is sometimes called "karma." Call it karma, or attribute it to the Biblical principle of "reaping what you sow," either way the reality of life that we all have seen and will continue to see is that "what goes around comes around." Our Higher Power, or the powers that be, will ALWAYS exact justice. We may not see it or have any hand in it, but it will happen and we can trust that. Those who do wrong will have consequences to walk out, some day. We can let it go and trust that it will be handled, and focus on our own journey to peace and happiness.

I want to be clear with you about this step of the process. If you do not fully release your hurt, your trauma, your pain, your anger, your bitterness, or any other toxic emotion that has been attached to your wounds, you will not be able to walk into freedom. You will not have fully forgiven. You will, in effect, still be chained to the floor of your trauma site, surrounded by the iron bars of your prison. So you can half-way do this thing if you want to, but I can promise you freedom will not be found for you. I get a lot of flak for being an "all-or-nothing" person in many areas of my life, but I will tell you that the only way to freedom is to attack your trauma with that exact philosophy. Either you do it ALL, or you might as well do nothing. Again, it's life or death. How badly do you want to LIVE?? This may take time (it is a *process)* but keep working at it until you get there. DO NOT GIVE UP.

Letting go, much like forgiving, sounds easier than it actually is. It really is an act of will, a choice, but the act of doing it is often a struggle. There are many ways to go about it. You can just resolve and say in your spirit, "I let him/her and all the pain attached to what they did go." Or maybe it needs to be more tangible for you, so writing it down could be helpful. One way I have done this: write down what and/or who I am releasing on paper, then destroy and throw the paper away. Another option is to write a letter to the person, then burn it. You can even write it on a balloon and release it to the atmosphere. There really is no right or wrong way to do it. The most important thing is that you are able, through whatever method you choose, to actually completely let it go and not continue to hold on to any part of it somewhere deep within.

When you fully let go you should feel lighter. I don't just mean emotionally or spiritually, I mean PHYSICALLY. I've not once done this or had someone else do this without there being an actual physiological response. It's as if we carry these things like physical weights inside us somehow, and when we release them we FEEL the loss of that weight. For me, often my shoulders suddenly don't seem as weighted down. Or maybe my chest feels less restricted as I breathe. Or maybe it's a barely discernable lightness about my whole being that I suddenly become aware of. Regardless of how you detect this, pay close attention...you should feel some kind of positive difference in your very being.

As you begin to release your hold on the people who have hurt you, and you release your hold on the pain that you carry with you, you are losing spiritual weight, so to speak. You will begin to walk with a joy and a lightness you've never had before. You will begin to experience peace on a level you've never experienced before. With each step, you will walk a little more into freedom.

To *Pray*
is to let go
and let God take over.
-Philippians 4:6-7

Chapter Six:
Being at Peace with One Another....

My mother taught me to live by this beautiful poem, called

"Desiderata." In this poem, written by Max Ehrmann, you find

instructions on how to live a good and happy life. He instructs us to

work to be at peace with all people in his line, "as far as possible

without surrender, be on good terms with all persons,"(1948). My

mom did an excellent job of living by this ideal and she certainly

instilled a desire in me to do the same. I have never liked conflict,

really, although I won't shy away from it when it's necessary. I

prefer to get along with everyone and work things out amicably wherever possible. When it isn't possible, my spirit feels terribly grieved, and that feeling of unrest is something that haunts me. For me to be at peace, I really do prefer to be at peace with all others. I truly try to live by this, but of course I will never be perfect in it.

I'm not sure why exactly, maybe because of my desire to have peace with all people, but something about the forgiving process also caused me to self-examine. Every time I forgave someone my conscience was pricked by some wrong I myself had perpetrated. So, I ended up doing a dual-process of forgiving others and asking for forgiveness for myself. I took a fearless moral inventory of myself throughout my life, from my earliest memory forward, and made another list. On this list I wrote all of the things I had done wrong that I felt I needed to ask forgiveness for or make amends for. Many of them I just asked my Higher Power to forgive me for without ever speaking to another person. Others, however, I felt strongly led to actually make direct amends for. I went so far back I had to track someone down I had known since kindergarten but had lost touch with since my school years. This person remembered me, but had no recollection of my "wrong." However, my conscience was cleared because I know I apologized and asked for forgiveness anyway. I acknowledged my wrongdoing and did what I could to make it right. In doing these two things....both forgiving and asking forgiveness...I found a sense of peace I'd not known in.....well, maybe ever. I found peace with all people. I won't tell you how to live your life, but I will say that I feel this degree of peace is important in living a happy and healthy life.

If you are a religious person, most religions include some form of atonement, making amends, or asking forgiveness in their belief system. If you are in recovery, most twelve-step programs include a "making amends" step. If you are a Christian, asking forgiveness and forgiving are both mandates.

Biblical scriptures on forgiveness:

"If you forgive those who sin against you, your heavenly Father will forgive you. But if you refuse to forgive others, your Father will not forgive your sins" (Matthew 6: 14-15NLT).

"Make allowance for each other's faults, and forgive anyone who offends you. Remember, the Lord forgave you, so you must forgive others" (Colossians 3:13 NLT).

"If we confess our sins, he is faithful and just to forgive us our sins, and to cleanse us from all unrighteousness" (1 John 1:9 KJV).

"If my people, who are called by my name, will humble themselves and pray and seek my face and turn from their wicked ways, then I will hear from heaven, and I will forgive their sin and will heal their land" (2 Chronicles 7:14 NIV).

Even if you are not a person of faith, however, I would challenge you to try forgiving others AND making your wrongs right. You won't regret it, and you will be a better person for it. There is actually something to be said for living a life of faith, by the way. Dr. Harold Koenig, a certified psychiatrist, professor, and director at Duke University, has conducted over 25 research studies on the effects of a religious lifestyle on health. Koenig specifically focuses on the traditional religious faith practices of Christians and Jews, and his research shows that people who live a faith-based lifestyle have lower rates of divorce and suicide, cope better with stress overall, have much lower rates of depression and more quickly overcome depression when it does occur, live longer and healthier lives in general, require less and shorter hospitalization, have less risk of cardiovascular disease, lower blood pressure, and stronger immune systems as a whole (2011). So maybe following a faith is just plain good for you??

With or without faith, however, most people feel a sense of morality or ethics, either internal at birth or fostered by their culture and environment throughout their lives. This internal thermometer, of sorts, pricks the conscience when something perceived as wrong is perpetrated. This can range from conviction to guilt, and can bleed into shame. Guilt and shame are toxic to the body, just like unforgiveness. They cripple you in the race of life and will leave you crumpled on the sidelines watching the "worthier" pass you by to success. Some of the most common causes of relapse in recovery are resentment (unforgiveness), guilt, and shame. According to Brené Brown, shame is little more than a fear of disconnection. We feel shame around things we fear others will reject us over, judge us over, or disconnect with us over. The best cure for shame is vulnerability and transparency. When you put your most "shamed" items out for others to see and they accept you anyway, shame vanishes without a trace. It is really that simple! Making amends for the things you feel shame over, asking forgiveness, sharing them with someone you trust implicitly, will alleviate any guilt and contribute to the newfound inner peace you will have. Can you even imagine walking around the world without ANY hurts, resentment, guilt, or shame? Can you even imagine being that FREE?? Let me tell you, it is worth every step you will have to take to get there. Don't postpone your peace, start pursuing it today!

Desiderata

Go placidly amid the noise and haste,
and remember what peace there may be in silence.
As far as possible without surrender
be on good terms with all persons.
Speak your truth quietly and clearly;
and listen to others,
even the dull and the ignorant;
they too have their story.

Avoid loud and aggressive persons,
they are vexations to the spirit.
If you compare yourself with others,
you may become vain and bitter;
for always there will be greater and lesser persons than yourself.
Enjoy your achievements as well as your plans.

Keep interested in your own career, however humble;
it is a real possession in the changing fortunes of time.
Exercise caution in your business affairs;
for the world is full of trickery.
But let this not blind you to what virtue there is;
many persons strive for high ideals;
and everywhere life is full of heroism.

Be yourself.
Especially, do not feign affection.
Neither be cynical about love;
for in the face of all aridity and disenchantment
it is as perennial as the grass.

Take kindly the counsel of the years,
gracefully surrendering the things of youth.
Nurture strength of spirit to shield you in sudden misfortune.
But do not distress yourself with dark imaginings.
Many fears are born of fatigue and loneliness.
Beyond a wholesome discipline,
be gentle with yourself.

You are a child of the universe,
no less than the trees and the stars;
you have a right to be here.
And whether or not it is clear to you,
no doubt the universe is unfolding as it should.

Therefore be at peace with God,
whatever you conceive Him to be,
and whatever your labors and aspirations,
in the noisy confusion of life keep peace with your soul.

With all its sham, drudgery, and broken dreams,
it is still a beautiful world.
Be cheerful.
Strive to be happy.

Max Ehrmann, Desiderata, Copyright 1952.

PRAYER CONCERNING MY OWN PERSONAL SINS

(Developed by Pastor Ronnie Hesters)

ISA 1:18 LORD, FORGIVE ME FOR MY OWN PERSONAL SINS, NOT ONLY AGAINST YOU, BUT

ALSO MY SINS AGAINST OTHERS.

Pray and ask the Holy Spirit to bring to remembrance any sin(s) that He has chosen to reveal

(no matter how long ago it was). Write them down as He brings them up and for each sin

Pray this prayer:

ISA 61:1 DEAR LORD, PLEASE FORGIVE ME, IN THE NAME OF JESUS, FOR ___NAME THE SIN.

I BREAK THE **POWER** OF THIS SIN OFF OF ME BY THE BLOOD OF JESUS!"

ACTS 16:23, 33 *Concerning sin against others, make restitution wherever possible and apologies when necessary.*

JOHN 8:37, 36 HEAVENLY FATHER, I THANK YOU FOR FORGIVING ME AND I FORGIVE MYSELF. BY

THE POWERFUL BLOOD OF JESUS I BREAK ALL CONTROL THAT THE DEVIL HAS

HAD OVER MY EMOTIONS IN THE AREAS OF GUILT,
SHAME, FEAR, SELF-

REJECTION, AND CONDEMNATION.

II PET 1:3-4   FATHER, I THANK YOU THAT YOU MADE ALL
THIS POSSIBLE FOR ME BY THE

WORK OF THE CROSS.

Repentance Worksheet:

People I need to apologize to:	Offense I committed:
1	
2	
3	
4	
5	
6	
7	
8	
9	
10	
11	
12	
13	
14	
15	
16	
17	
18	
19	
20	

Repentance Worksheet:

Offenses I committed:	Way I can make amends:
1	
2	
3	
4	
5	
6	
7	
8	
9	
10	
11	
12	
13	
14	
15	
16	
17	
18	
19	
20	

<u>Sample Repentance Prayer:</u>

Dear Heavenly Father,

Please forgive me for _____. I know it was wrong and I am sorry. I don't ever want to do that again. Please help me to turn away from that behavior and never repeat it. Thank you for forgiving me, for dying on the cross for my sins, and for loving me in spite of them. I love you.

In Jesus' Name,

Amen

Chapter Seven: Rebuilding Yourself.....

Chances are that you have allowed yourself to be defined by your abuse, by your abuser(s), and by your life circumstances in some ways. If not in an obvious way, then at least in that you have since filtered the world through skewed lenses, spectacles placed on your eyes by those people or events. Let me give you a personal example of what I mean by this.

I was rejected as an infant, even before birth, by my biological father. Was that my fault? Was I such an atrocious little being that my own flesh and blood couldn't bear to be near me? Of course not!! But somewhere deep inside me, that is exactly what I believed. I bought that lie hook, line, and sinker. I saw the world from that moment on through the lens of rejection. I expected everyone around me to reject me. I was grateful if they did not. I would go to great lengths to be likeable, loveable, "worthy" of their attention, and to keep everyone around me happy, for fear that I would be rejected again. I believed I had to earn love and acceptance by my actions, and sometimes my appearance. I believed that I alone was not enough. I was not worthy to be loved.

So as others came into my life and abused me, instead of rebelling against their abuse and criticism I molded myself to it. I became whatever they wanted me to be, or said they wanted me to be, to try to avoid the abuse, and to avoid rejection. What do you think happened? It's obvious I suppose. I found myself at the age of 30, an absolutely lost shell of a person. I didn't even know who I was!! I had "become" this person who was not me, was not who I wanted to be, and still those around me were not happy. And I, least of all.

This epiphany spurred in me a desire to discover myself. What a grand exploration it was! I have enjoyed the great archaeological dig of the last decade, and I can say that I now know myself. I like myself. In fact, I even love myself! And never again will I allow anyone else to "change" me. With the help of my Higher Power, God, I have rebuilt myself from the ground up. I have gone back to my true self. I am comfortable in my own skin. I live a life true to myself these days. As should you!!

I throw down a gauntlet before you today. I challenge you to find your way back to yourself. To get to know yourself, to come to love yourself. To live your life authentically as the one true YOU, as no one else on this planet can ever do. Only you can be you! You are worthy of love. You are worthy of belonging. Yours is a life worthy to be lived.

"Only by getting in touch with your body, by connecting viscerally with yourself, can you regain a sense of who you are, your priorities and values," (van der Kolk 2014, p. 249). The first step is practicing self-awareness and working to become more conscious of yourself in practical ways on a day to day basis. Reconnect with yourself, physically and emotionally. Then you can truly begin to rediscover who you truly are at your core.

How do you rediscover yourself? It takes a great deal of introspection. Exploration. Trial and error. What are the things you once loved but have long since forgotten? Pull those things out of the attic, go do those things. What are the bits of you that you used to be proud of? Things you thought you might even be good at? Go do those things!! What are the qualities you most admire in humanity, and in others? Start demonstrating those qualities. Start trying new things. Read new books. Life is a grand adventure, and it's time you started enjoying it! Develop some new hobbies, things you really find give you a sense of fulfillment, accomplishment, peace, and joy. Anything that brings you those feelings, do those things! Before you know it, you will be remembering who you are...just you wait and see....

Uncovering Faulty Beliefs:

In EMDR (Eye Movement Desensitization and Reprocessing), as developed by Francine Shapiro, a goal of therapy is to discover or uncover untrue core beliefs, referred to as "negative cognitions," and to replace those beliefs with "positive cognitions" or TRUTH (2018). Some of the most common cognitions are as follows:

Negative Cognition	Positive Cognition
I'm worthless	I'm worthy
I'm a bad person	I'm a good person
I'm not loveable	I'm loveable
I'm powerless	I'm powerful
I'm in danger	I'm safe now
I can't succeed	I can succeed
I'm not enough	I am enough
I am weak	I am strong
It is my fault	I did my best
I can't trust anyone	I can choose who to trust
I am going to die	I am safe now, I'm alive
I am not in control	I am in control now
I am not good enough	I am good enough
I am broken	I am whole

If you'd like to seek the help of your Higher Power in revealing faulty beliefs or lies that have infiltrated your core belief system as a result of hurts or trauma, feel free to do so. An example prayer is included below, take liberties to reword as you feel led:

Seek Spiritual Assistance in Uncovering False Beliefs:

LORD, I ASK YOU TO REVEAL TO ME ALL OF **SATAN'S LIES** CONCERNING THE

MEMORIES ASSOCIATED WITH MY HURTS. (EX: SELF-CONDEMNATION)

(PRAY AND LISTEN, THEN WRITE THEM DOWN)

Faulty Beliefs

There are likely false beliefs about yourself and the world that you have taken on, maybe unknowingly, as a result of things done to you or experienced by you. This rebuilding period is a time of introspection and examination. Search for those beliefs, those *lies*, and confront them with TRUTH. The main types of beliefs to search for are:

1. Beliefs about yourself (your worth, your value, your ability to be loved, your ability to function and be successful, etc.).

2. Beliefs about the world in general (are all people untrustworthy, is everyone against you, etc.).

3. Beliefs about the relationship between yourself and the world (are you "different," is it possible for you to "belong," are you "irretrievably broken," no one will ever want you, etc.).

*What is your TRUTH??

I am loveable. I am worthy. I deserve respect. I deserve happiness.

BELIEFS WORKSHEET:

FALSE BELIEF/LIE	TRUTH
Ex:I am unlovable.	*Ex:I am LOVEABLE.*

Chapter Eight: Taking Your Power Back...

If you have experienced abuse or personal trauma, you know what it is like to feel helpless....worthless...***powerless***. As a child, when an adult coerces you, manipulates you, or forces you to engage in sexual behaviors....you feel pretty powerless. You feel that it doesn't really matter in those moments what you want or need; you have to just go along with what you know you are supposed to do. When someone hits you or causes you physical harm, and they are bigger and stronger than you, you are powerless to stop them. Any attempt to do so is futile. When your parent or caregiver screams your uselessness at you, what power do you have to stop them? None. These are just a few examples of an unlimited number of ways in which we have been or can be harmed and are powerless to protect ourselves. In those instances, and many others, we feel powerless. They have taken our power from us. Sometimes that feeling of powerlessness stays with us long beyond that single incident. I know that is how it was for me, at least. I felt my ability to say what I wanted to be done to me, or with my life, was taken from me. I just had to let things happen to me as they came, and there wasn't much I could do about it. Or so I *believed*. Those people took our power without our permission, against our will, and maybe we unknowingly let them KEEP IT. Why would we do that??? Because we don't know any better. When we hold on to our anger, unforgiveness, bitterness, and resentment against those who have hurt us, we are also letting those people have power over us. There is a saying common in 12-step programs, "Don't let them live rent-free in your head." When we hold within us those negative feelings toward someone, we think about those people and the wrongs they committed, we obsess at times, even, and that negativity begins to consume us. It is so powerful it is controlling how we think, what decisions we make, whether we have peace, and how we enjoy our day to day lives. We have given them total power over us. Do they deserve that??? OF COURSE NOT!!! Not only did those people not deserve to have our power in the moments they hurt us, but they certainly don't deserve our power for one second longer than that. We have to examine ourselves, honestly and thoroughly, and determine if anyone, anywhere has any unwarranted power over us that they do not need or deserve. I don't know about you, but I don't want ANYONE to have power over me except ME. Once you have recognized and acknowledged where that power lies, do what you need to do to TAKE YOUR POWER BACK.

That probably will mean forgiving those who have hurt you and choosing to let it go, for good. Forgive them, release them, and bless them, as we discussed in chapter four. Why would I discuss this twice in the same book? Because it is CRUCIAL! If you want to have agency over your own body and your own life, you have to make sure you have not willingly given power to anyone else. Now, to have the best life, give your power to your Higher Power. But no human on earth needs or deserves it!

Another important aspect of taking your power back is to allow yourself to be vulnerable and transparent with others in order to smash the shame and guilt underneath your heels as you walk into your future. Stop hiding in the shadows and keeping the secrets of your abusers. Stop protecting THEM. They certainly didn't protect YOU! I don't mean to be vindictive or to tell everyone you know about what they did to you. Rather, be your true authentic self and don't be afraid to share your story for fear of upsetting them or harming them in some way. In appropriate settings, share your story. BREAK THE SILENCE. "Silence about trauma also leads to death—the death of the soul," (van der Kolk 2014, p. 234). Journal your story. Write your story in poems, write it in songs, write it in prose. Speak your story out via some method. This is a powerful move for you to make. Scary, I know. Believe me, I know! Be wise about how you share, do not put yourself in harm's way, but find ways to break your silence at last.

Once you have made sure there are no remnants of someone else's power over you because of your own choices, look around you. Are you allowing others to have undue influence over you? Do you people-please beyond what is healthy or desirable for you? Do you put other's needs and wants above your own to your own physical and emotional detriment? Are you doing certain things in your life only to keep someone else happy, or because they "advised" you to? If any of these are true, ask yourself why this is the case. Are you ready to take charge and be your own boss? Are you ready to take your power back? Only you can choose to and act on it. But whenever you are ready, you CAN.

Educate yourself on what a healthy relationship looks like and start to work to make the relationships around you healthier (see information at the end of this chapter). Work on toxic, unhealthy behaviors and patterns in you and those around you. Distance yourself from people who do not have your best interests at heart, and who do not seem to respect the new, healthier boundaries you set. Love yourself enough to create a healthy inner circle for yourself, where you can set limits and take care of yourself without incurring anger or backlash from "friends" and loved ones. Once you are able to do this you will begin to better discern unhealthy relationships as they form and will be able to keep your inner circle happy and healthy, and hopefully avoid getting entangled in any abusive relationships in the future. Remember that you ARE in control of your own life, and no one has power over you unless you allow them that. When you were a child you may not have had much choice, but today you have ALL the choice! The decision of how to use the choices before you is yours, and YOUR TIME starts now!

"It's time to take your life back from the people that are causing you pain and making you unhappy. This is your life and you are the author of your story. If you're stuck on the same page, just remember that at any moment...you have the power to write a new chapter."

-Robert Tew

PRAYER OF DELIVERANCE FROM THE POWER OF THOSE WHO HAVE HURT ME

(Developed by Pastor Ronnie Hesters)

REV 12:11   LORD JESUS, BY THE POWER OF YOUR SHED BLOOD, AND BECAUSE OF THE FACT

1 JOHN 3:1   THAT I AM YOUR SON/DAUGHTER, WITH ALL RIGHTS AND PRIVILAGES OF A CHILD

OF THE KING, I TAKE THE AUTHORITY THAT YOU HAVE GIVEN ME—IN YOUR NAME,

1 PET 5:7-9   THE NAME OF JESUS, I CANCEL AND DESTROY ALL OF SATAN'S AUTHORITY AND

POWER OVER ME IN THESE MEMORIES OF PAIN.

NOW, LORD, I SAY AGAIN, BY THE PRECIOUS BLOOD OF JESUS, I SMASH AND

II COR 10:4-5   DESTROY ALL OF SATAN'S STRONGHOLDS IN MY MIND, EMOTIONS, AND IN ALL

MY BITTER MEMORIES.

In Jesus' Name, AMEN!!

Ways to Address Violators/Abusers Safely:

It often is not safe to have contact of any kind with our abusers. It also may not even be possible (they could be unknown entities, in unknown locations, or deceased). There are several ways we can address our wounds directly and specifically with them without having any contact. One is to write them a letter. You will destroy or burn the letter afterward; the point is not to get the letter to them but to process and let go of the pain they caused you. Write a letter to them saying all the things you feel you need to say, perhaps read it aloud, and then destroy it. Another option is to find a way to say out loud what you need to….either to an empty chair, to their headstone, to a photograph of them, a drawing or painting that represents them, or using your imagination. There is no danger of repercussion because they are not actually present during this. A final option is to allow your therapist, a close friend, or other person to be a "stand in" for your abuser and to say what you need to say to that person in a safe environment. In doing any of the above exercises, here are some guidelines that would be helpful for you to follow:

1. Express how you felt when they did what they did, how angry and/or hurt you were, and be as vocal and animated as you need to be. Remember to give yourself permission to FEEL whatever it is you feel. Do not repress or shame yourself for your emotions. This is YOUR TIME.

2. Tell them what you needed and wanted from them instead of what happened. Express any unmet needs to them, failed expectations of them, or losses in your life as a result of what happened.

3. Tell them what basic beliefs or values of yours (and/or society's) they violated in doing what they did. You have a right to be safe and loved, for example.

4. Tell them what you choose to do now. Maybe even from this moment forward. If you choose to forgive, let the pain go, take care of yourself, protect yourself,

make sure a similar thing never happens again, etc. This is you taking and declaring your power. Even if it's hard, do it. You deserve it. You need to know your own power to be whole and healthy. Declaring it out loud can be freeing---imagine the bars of your prison crumbling around you as you speak!

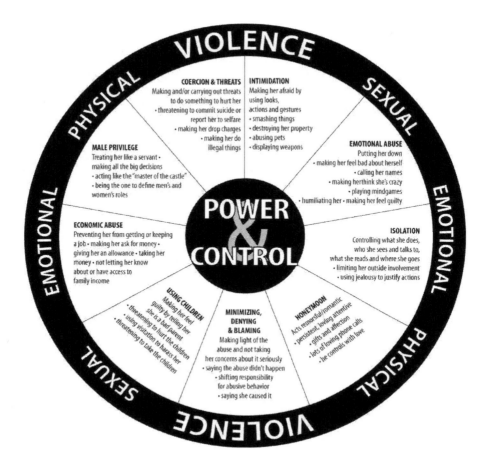

VIOLENCE

PHYSICAL

SEXUAL

EMOTIONAL

EMOTIONAL

PHYSICAL

SEXUAL

VIOLENCE

POWER & CONTROL

COERCION & THREATS
Making and/or carrying out threats to do something to hurt her • threatening to commit suicide or report her to selfare • making her drop charges • making her do illegal things

INTIMIDATION
Making her afraid by using looks, actions and gestures • smashing things • destroying her property • abusing pets • displaying weapons

MALE PRIVILEGE
Treating her like a servant • making all the big decisions • acting like the "master of the castle" • being the one to define men's and women's roles

EMOTIONAL ABUSE
Putting her down • making her feel bad about herself • calling her names • making her think she's crazy • playing mindgames • humiliating her • making her feel guilty

ECONOMIC ABUSE
Preventing her from getting or keeping a job • making her ask for money • giving her an allowance • taking her money • not letting her know about or have access to family income

ISOLATION
Controlling what she does, who she sees and talks to, what she reads and where she goes • limiting her outside involvement • using jealousy to justify actions

USING CHILDREN
Making her feel guilty by telling her she is a bad parent • threatening to hurt the children • using visitation to harass her • threatening to take the children

MINIMIZING, DENYING & BLAMING
Making light of the abuse and not taking her concerns about it seriously • saying the abuse didn't happen • shifting responsibility for abusive behavior • saying she caused it

HONEYMOON
Acts remorseful/romantic • persistent, loving attentive • gifts and affection • lots of loving phone calls • he controls with love

This diagram demonstrates the ways power and control can be used manipulatively and abusively in relationships. The use of power and control is never healthy and is a sign of an abusive person. Be wary of anyone who uses these methods in your life. Distance yourself from them for your own health.

Cycle of Abuse

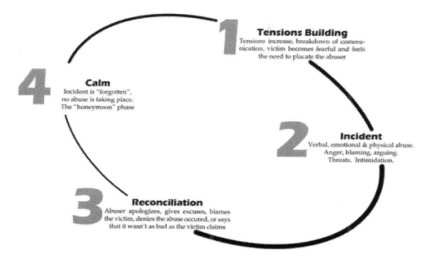

1 Tensions Building
Tensions increase, breakdown of communication, victim becomes fearful and feels the need to placate the abuser

4 Calm
Incident is "forgotten", no abuse is taking place. The "honeymoon" phase

2 Incident
Verbal, emotional & physical abuse. Anger, blaming, arguing. Threats. Intimidation.

3 Reconciliation
Abuser apologizes, gives excuses, blames the victim, denies the abuse occured, or says that it wasn't as bad as the victim claims

This is what is known as the "cycle of abuse." This pattern is very typical in abusive relationships. Abusive patterns can be present in friendships, parental relationships, work relationships, and intimate relationships. If you see this pattern occurring, it is not healthy and can escalate quickly and dangerously. Get out of the relationship if at all possible. Domestic violence is behind 47% of all family homicides (Ogrodnick 2008). Three women die in a domestic violence situation every single day (Ogrodnick 2008). GET OUT. See the resources in the back of this book for information that can help you get out safely and alive. Call 911 if you are in immediate danger. Call the **National Domestic Violence Hotline: 1-800-799-SAFE (7233)** to learn what local resources you have. Leaving a domestic violence situation is very dangerous and should be done with support and the aid of people who understand the dangers. You can get out and you can live a life of peace and safety. Love yourself enough.

Characteristics of a Healthy Relationship

- **Respect**-mutual acceptance of who each partner is, their autonomy, and their uniqueness
- **Honesty**-open and honest communication in all matters
- **Realistic expectations**-each partner is responsible for meeting their own needs and does not expect the other partner to do so
- **Trust**-each partner is trustworthy and also trusting
- **Autonomy**-Independent, autonomy, but sharing of that autonomy in intimacy
- **Shared Power**-mutual give and take, with neither partner being controlling
- **Tenderness**-a demonstration of physical affection, thoughtfulness, and consideration
- **Time**-spending quality time together and valuing time with one another
- **Long-Term Commitment**-the intention to be in the relationship long-term and to do whatever is possible to work things out when there are disagreements or difficulties
- **Forgiveness**-Remembering transgressions but forgiving them and letting them go. No one is perfect, neither you nor your partner, so there has to be room for mistakes to be made and forgiven within any relationship.

Chapter Nine: Healing the Memories.....

I believe one of the most difficult things for survivors to overcome is the haunting that takes place within the mind and body of the memories of what we have experienced. These memories stay with us everywhere we go. In the tension we carry in our bodies. In the anxiety we feel in our gut. In our inability to focus for constantly surveying our surroundings for signs of danger. In our dreams at night…oh, the horrible, vivid, terrifying dreams when our eyes close and our bodies attempt to find respite. In flashbacks that can hit us without warning at anytime, anywhere. In the "being taken back" we experience anytime we encounter a trigger, which could be a sound, a sight, a scent, a touch, a photograph, a song, a word…..well, it can be ANYTHING, really….and there we are, right back in the midst of the horror all over again. Are you getting the picture yet? The memories are WITH US. Everywhere we go. And here is the craziest part of all…they are WITH US even when we have blocked them out and deny that they even exist. There they are, just the same.

Finding a way to heal the memories is very important, though. Because if we don't find a way to heal them, then they will remain with us, terrorizing us, for the rest of our lives. Every person's journey is different, and I wish I knew a formula for just erasing them or taking all the pain out of them instantly. But I do not. I can, however, share with you things I have learned and tried that have helped heal mine.

I believe the biggest thing I have done is to forgive. I was once tormented with regular nightmares and flashbacks from one particular abuser, but when I forgave him and fully let go of all the pain, those symptoms immediately improved. I also asked my

Higher Power, who I call God, to remove the pain attached to the memories, and to sever any kind of connection I had with that person once and for all. I believe we are often spiritually attached in some way to our abusers, and breaking any kind of spiritual tie to them is a huge part of gaining our freedom from them. So, I forgave and broke my ties to him. Now, in the external world there was also a legal restraining order preventing him from ever contacting me, and there was no contact for over a decade. Then, life threw me a curveball….or God decided to test my healing, however you want to look at it.

After over a decade of no contact with this person, I was forced to see him again at a funeral. I had anxiety about the possibility of seeing him for days beforehand, but when I actually saw him again I felt no fear. NONE. I met his eyes from across a room and felt no rush of panic, as I expected. I didn't feel a rise of anxiety, or a racing heartbeat. Instead, I felt pity for him and the life he was wasting. That was one of the most freeing experiences of my life. To be face to face with an abuser (by the way, he attempted to kill me on more than one occasion) but to feel no fear because I knew he could no longer hurt me. He had no power over me in that moment whatsoever. And that level of freedom I gained just from forgiving him and cleansing myself spiritually.

Another method I have used and found to be effective is the use of writing to journal or process specific memories. I have done a lot of writing about my abuse and trauma history, including poetry, short stories, and even books. Writing has always been therapeutic for me but may not be for you. Find the things that work best for you and be creative in how to use those therapeutically for your own healing.

EMDR (Eye Movement Desensitization and Reprocessing) therapy is also something I have used and found to be healing. EMDR was actually designed specifically for working with traumatic and distressing memories. Traumatic memories do not get stored in the brain appropriately with other "normal" memories and are activated when triggered by something similar, sending the system into fight or flight mode. In EMDR you activate and aid your brain in processing traumatic memories so that they can be moved out of the part of the brain that causes them to easily be triggered and throw you back into survival mode. Once the memories are reprocessed and stored properly in the area where "normal" memories are stored, the anxiety, fear, triggering, etc., attached to those memories stops. EMDR has been found to be quite effective in treating PTSD and is currently one of the leading modalities. The other most commonly used treatment modalities are discussed in the back of this book, but here I will focus on EMDR because that is the one I personally have had the most success with in both my own healing and in my clinical work with individuals recovering from trauma.

The Department of Defense/Department of Veterans Affairs Practice Guidelines have listed EMDR in the highest-ranking category for treatment, recommended for trauma populations at all times (2017). The American Psychiatric Association Practice Guideline (2004) states that SSRIs, CBT, and EMDR are all recommended as first-line treatments of trauma. The International Society for Traumatic Stress Studies' treatment guidelines has also listed EMDR as an effective treatment modality for PTSD (Foa, Keane, Friedman, & Cohen 2009). Trauma-focused CBT and

EMDR are the only psychotherapies recommended for children, adolescents, and adults with PTSD by the World Health Organization (2013).

EMDR may be preferred among the various professional organizations for several reasons. Similar to trauma-focused CBT, EMDR is successful in reducing subjective distress as well as strengthening adaptive cognitions related to the traumatic event, however EMDR alone does not involve any re-traumatizing exposure to the event, detailed descriptions of the event ("re-living" of it), any direct challenging of beliefs, or homework (World Health Organization 2013). It appears to be the most effective and efficient therapy model used at this time. EMDR is formatted in such a way that the therapist's own biases do not come into play in any significant way, the client/patient is his/her own proponent and processes at their own pace in their own way with little to no guidance from the therapist. The client/patient does not have to disclose to the therapist what the traumatic event or memory being reprocessed is, in fact the therapist needs to know very little of the situation in order to help the client reprocess the memory. The issues are generally resolved in one session, although some more complex or deeper traumas can take multiple sessions. Because of the style of EMDR approach, it tends to involve the least amount of present discomfort for the quickest complete resolution.

If you decide to try this style of therapy, make sure you find an experienced EMDR-trained therapist who has worked extensively with trauma patients. The more experienced they are, the better therapy will generally go for you. And if you find it isn't a good fit after trying it, that's okay. Don't stop pursuing your healing, as there are a myriad of styles and methods that address traumatic memories out there.

If you choose any other type of therapy, I highly recommend finding a therapist who uses that model who is also "trauma-focused," as it is crucial that the therapist working with you understands how trauma affects you within the clinical setting. You also want to be comfortable with the therapist you chose to work with. If you are not comfortable or don't feel safe with them, then keep looking until you find one who is a good fit for you. You are in charge of your own treatment and have the right to choose what works best for you, including who you seek therapy from. I think going to your Higher Power for guidance is an excellent place to start in this area. Remember that healing takes courage and work, but isn't it worth it to be totally free and be able to fully enjoy your life? Don't you deserve that? Of course you do!!

PRAYER OF HEALING FOR MEMORIES

LORD JESUS, I ASK YOU TO FORGIVE ME FOR ALL THE TOXIC EMOTIONS ABOUT WHAT HAPPENED

1 JOHN 1:4   THAT I HAVE BEEN CARRYING IN MY HEART FOR SO LONG AGAINST __NAME__:

THOUGHTS OF UNFORGIVENESS, ANGER, BITTERNESS, RESENTMENT, RETALIATION, SHAME AND FEAR.

HEB 12:15   LORD, HELP ME TO NOT REPLAY THOSE HURTFUL MEMORIES IN MY MIND.

LORD, I ASK YOU TO HEAL THE HURT AND BROKENNESS THAT IS IN MY HEART.

LUKE 4:18   RIGHT NOW, LORD, I LIFT THIS PAIN UP TO YOU. TAKE MY PAIN AND MY MEMORIES, JESUS. GIVE ME FREEDOM FROM THIS BONDAGE.

EPH 4:23   I ASK YOU TO RENEW MY MIND AND PURGE MY CONSCIENCE FROM

HEB 9:14   ALL THOSE POLLUTING MEMORIES THAT HAVE TORMENTED ME FOR SO LONG.

In Jesus' Name,

AMEN

Chapter Ten: Healing Your Body.....

Trauma "does a number" to your body. Bessel van der Kolk talks about the body "keeping the score." This is true, as I can attest from my own personal experience. My body stored the memories of the trauma in my very muscle, and in my brain. I used to get triggered by the tiniest little thing, and my whole body would go into fight or flight before I even understood what was happening. Sometimes it would take me days or even months to figure out what it was that triggered me. It is not at all a conscious reaction, but most unconscious and instinctual. Years of staying in fight or flight left my body perpetually exhausted. My adrenal system was fatigued, my immune system weakened, my blood pressure was high, and my entire body stayed tense, particularly my upper shoulders and neck area. There was trauma that occurred directly to my shoulders and neck, and they wouldn't fully relax no matter how hard I tried. My body refused to forget what my mind could not even remember. We can't change what was done to our bodies. I am fully aware of this. But I maintain that there are definitive things we can do to start the healing process for our physical selves as well as our emotional, mental, and spiritual selves.

The core of recovery is self-awareness (van der Kolk 2014). Start by working to become more aware of your body, different sensations, tension, pain, and discomfort. Traumatized people often have tightness in their chest, tension in their body, unbearable sensations in their stomachs, and they teach themselves to become unaware of these things just to cope day to day (van der Kolk 2014). Try doing a body scan: start with your head and slowly work your way down your body, all the way to your toes, noticing each body part as you go and seeing if you can detect any unusual sensations you may have been previously unaware of. I would even recommend trying to do a body scan several times a day, to get into the habit of being more aware of your own body.

Begin to practice mindfulness, being fully present in each moment, and making a point to notice yourself and the things around you. Think of the saying "take time to smell the roses," and start trying to live your life that way. There is no hurry, no rush, to get everywhere you are going. Slow your pace down and start noticing the little things. This may take fighting your urge to distract or get lost in your mind, but it is worth the work it may take to learn a new way of being. This will help you be more self-aware and simultaneously will begin to help you shift out of fight or flight by calming the sympathetic nervous system. It really does work!

One of the after-effects of trauma is the tendency toward self-destruction. It's as if we believe, because others have treated us as though we have no value as living beings, that we inherently don't deserve to live. So, we set about destroying ourselves in sometimes subtle, and other times not so subtle, ways. Some common examples of this are: eating disorders, self-mutilation, reckless driving, substance abuse, self-sabotaging, risky sexual behavior, excessive spending, and other addictive or dangerous behaviors. I've been guilty of a few of those, how about you?

If we are going to truly accept and love ourselves, part of that is taking good care of ourselves. Instead of abusing ourselves, which is essentially following in the footsteps of our abusers, we need to love ourselves back to health. What can you do to be healthier? Do you have some self-destructive habits you would like to abandon? If you don't think you can do it on your own, seek help. There is no shame in that! Find a counselor or therapist who can support you in that process, and who can also point you to helpful resources you may not even know about. Reach out to some of your friends and ask them to be a support person, or maybe an accountability partner, in helping you change those behaviors. They love you--they won't mind!

In addition to changing our behavior patterns and unhealthy coping mechanisms, there are some basic tenants to healthy living that we may be neglecting. This may seem elementary, but as someone who was in an abusive relationship, I know that it is all too common for even the simplest things to be neglected. If you have not had a medical checkup within the last year, it's past time. Go get a general exam to make sure there are not any looming issues that can be easily treated if caught in time. Living in a high-stress environment, and likely in flight-or-fight mode, increases your chances of having some underlying health issues. Take care of them, take care of yourself--you have a wonderful life that's about to begin! It's time to rise up out of that hole they dug for you and stand as the person you deserve to be. You deserve to be cared for in every way!

Another often-neglected area is dental care. If you have not had a dental check-up in the last year, please go as soon as possible. If cost is an issue, most areas offer low-cost or free clinics a few times a year. Small colleges or technical schools with dental programs often offer free training clinics where their students perform free dental work in order to gain experience. Use the infamous google to find out what resources are near you and take advantage of them! I also recommend researching natural health options as a possible alternative in many cases, so you may want to do a little research before potentially having an unnecessary procedure done. Use your best judgement, just don't neglect yourself any longer.

The other things I want to address are part of a healthy lifestyle and will require thought and action on a daily basis. If you have medical issues that recommend or require a special diet, but you have not been following this diet, love yourself enough to make wise decisions. If you do not have medical issues affecting your diet, thank your Higher Power and take steps to ensure that things stay that way! Make healthy eating choices as often as you can. Eat organic foods when possible, eat foods low in sugar, with as little processing as possible, foods low in fat, rule out anything artificial, eat whole foods as the bulk of your diet, and start taking a daily supplement (Consumer Reports 2017). These are just simple guidelines that can make a difference in your health and how you feel very quickly. Remember, this is about LOVING YOURSELF enough to take care of yourself. YOU ARE WORTH IT!

Exercise is also an important part of living a healthy life. Start to incorporate that as much as you can. Small changes can make a big difference. It can be as little as 7 to 10 minutes a day, or even 30 minutes once or twice a week, but start somewhere. Walking is a great way to start. Get some fresh air, a little sunshine, and start making your heart stronger. You will feel so much better!

Part of healing your body is healing your mind. If you have a history of trauma or abuse, I strongly recommend that you seek therapy. It is nothing to be ashamed of. It is just like going to the medical doctor....you are treating your emotional and psychological health. I consider it a part of being holistically healthy. I am a therapist, and I go to therapy, too!! The work I have done in therapy has been an integral part of my healing process, and I cannot put that in words on paper for you to read and apply on your own. That has to be done individually in session between you and the therapist of your choice. I have found both traditional talk therapy and EMDR therapy to be helpful in reducing my PTSD symptoms, especially my being triggered by trivial events that just occur in daily life. There is a more in-depth discussion on the various therapies recommended for treating trauma in the back of this book. Healing is not limited to the techniques I have experience with and I encourage you to explore and find what works best for you! Using the methods I discuss here…forgiveness, treating myself holistically, using spiritual guidance, and traditional psychotherapy as well as EMDR, have brought me a long way on my healing journey. I am very functional with little to no anxiety, depression, or fear now. I once was plagued with panic attacks, nightmares, chronic debilitating anxiety, and was in a perpetual state of fear for my life. If you can relate, please know you don't have to stay that way! Apply the principles I discuss in this book and continue to seek help in overcoming those things. It can be done!

"Until you heal the wounds of your past, you are going to bleed. You can bandage the bleeding with food, with alcohol, with drugs, with work, with cigarettes, with sex; but eventually, it will all ooze through and stain your life. You must find the strength to open the wounds, stick your hands inside, pull out the core of the pain that is holding you in your past, the memories and make peace with them." -Ivanla Vanzant

As discussed in an earlier chapter, faith can play a large role in your ability to attain true wholeness and health. As I have stated, your spirit is an integral part of who you are as a person and you must nourish and feed your spirit in order to be a truly healthy and whole person. This idea may seem invalid on the surface, but research actually demonstrates the difference practicing faith can make in a person's health. Dr. Harold Koenig, a psychiatrist and professor at Duke University, has conducted numerous studies on the effects of various religious practices and human health (2011). Of 125 studies he found that in 85 of those studies people who attended church regularly were found to live longer than their counterparts (Koenig 2011). Further, Dr. Koenig reports that an article published in the Southern Medical Journal found that prayer had a significant effect on patients with hearing and visual deficiencies, literally improving them in discernable ways evident in audio and visual tests (Koenig 2011). Dr. Koenig sums up his research in this statement, "The benefits of devout religious practice, particularly involvement in a faith community and religious commitment, are that people cope better. In general, they cope with stress better, they experience greater well-being because they have more hope, they're more optimistic, they experience less depression, less anxiety, and they commit suicide less often. They have stronger immune systems, lower blood pressure, and probably better cardiovascular functioning," (Koenig 2011). Tom Knox, an atheist who converted to faith after conducting an in-depth study of the medical benefits of faith, says of his research, "What I discovered astonished me. Over the past 30 years a growing and largely unnoticed body of scientific work shows religious belief is medically, socially, and psychologically beneficial," (Newsmax Health 2018).

My question is if science demonstrates faith to be a healthier lifestyle in general, why reject it? And with that choice, how do you plan to nourish your spirit? I confronted myself with that question many years ago, and I chose faith. I firmly believe without my faith I would not be alive today. I'm not prescribing my choice to you, but.....you are a *spiritual being* and I will challenge you today to acknowledge that and decide for yourself how you will live a spiritual life and nourish that monumental part of yourself. Your health demands it! 😊

Let me tell you a little story…..

There really are two possible scenarios in life. One is that faith is a human idea generated in weakness and fantasy that has no value, and the other is that faith, in fact, is valid and real. So, let's look at both of these scenarios for a moment. Let's say, for example, you have a Christian believer who has a strong faith on the one hand, and you have a devout atheist who denies any value in faith on the other hand. Scenario one would purport that the atheist, who believes in no God, no Heaven, and no Hell, and has lived his or her life according to his or her own wishes, desires, and ethics, dies and just ceases to exist, as do all people if his or her belief system is correct. There is no punishment for the atheist for not following a set of beliefs. However, when the Christian in this scenario dies, they, too, simply cease to exist. There is no reward as they had so hoped, but there is also no punishment. The atheist and the Christian meet identical fates.

In the second scenario, though, the Christian believer has seen the real value in faith, and when they die they will go to the glorious Heaven they believe in and have so longed for. In this same scenario, what happens to the atheist? The atheist, unfortunately, will perish for lack of a belief system. He or she will miss out on the wonder and beauty of Heaven and will possibly be tortured throughout all of eternity for this oversight of faith. So, in the first scenario, no one benefits and no one suffers. But in the second scenario it is a completely different story. So, what is the benefit, I ask you, of holding on devoutly to the absence of a belief system? Is there any benefit at all??

Just food for thought……..

Chapter Eleven: Embracing ALL of you.....

Another important aspect of healing, I believe, is acceptance. Ultimately, we must follow the tenants of the Serenity Prayer so often used in twelve-step meetings, "*God, grant me the serenity to accept the things I cannot change, the courage to change the things I can, and the wisdom to know the difference.*" Some things about our existence we can change....how much we let our "triggers" affect us, how much we allow ourselves to be controlled by fear, how much of our future we allow to be dictated by our past, and how aggressively we fight for our freedom. Some things, however, we cannot change: what happened to us. We must come to a place of acceptance that we cannot change what happened, and it is now a part of who we are. It is a part of who we are, but it does not DEFINE us.

It is important to know that we cannot separate what happened to us from the people we are today. I experienced severe physical trauma to my neck as a young girl. I want to forget that trauma, and to erase it would be nice at times, but the reality is I still have some physical after-effects of that event that I am very aware of every single day. To forget I'd have to have a new neck. I can't very well cut off my neck and go buy a replacement! So, I must accept that the neck I have now, post-incident, is the neck I will always have. I do what I can to keep it as functional and healthy as I can, but I know I cannot make it "new" again. Regular visits to my chiropractor help alleviate the pain and discomfort that are still remnants for me, but my neck is curved in ways that are unnatural and that can't be corrected. I accept that! That's okay! I am still a happy, healthy, WHOLE person, and I do not allow that trauma to my neck to in any way define who I am or how I choose to live my life.

Let me give you another example, a more emotional one. My ex-husband often called me derogatory names, belittled me, criticized me, and would shove me, physically throw me through the air, strangle me, and punch me if I did not do exactly what he wanted to his satisfaction. After some time of this treatment I began to believe I was useless, worthless, sub-intelligent, and an inconvenience to everyone who knew me. I began to think death would be a welcome reprieve, not just for me but for everyone I "burdened." I was allowing his opinion of me, and his abusive behavior, to define my self-worth. After leaving that relationship, over time I began to see that I do, in fact, have innate value and worth just as a person, apart from what I do or don't do. Even if I'm imperfect. Even when I make mistakes. I began to believe I have a reason to live and that some people are glad I am alive. In reality no one is actually "burdened" by my existence. I stopped letting those things define me. They never really did! It was actually a mindgame perpetrated on me by my abuser to destroy me emotionally and make me ever more dependent on him.

Today, I accept that I was a victim of domestic violence. I was abused, but that does not make me a victim. Today I am a SURVIVOR, and that is a whole other thing! I will no longer be defined by what he did to me. In fact, I have worked diligently, using many of the principles outlined in this book in addition to individual counseling, to overcome the after-effects of that abuse in my mind and my body. I no longer have panic attacks out of fear that he will find me and kill me. I no longer jump at the sound of my name. I no longer shake inside when a man looks at me from across a room, or approaches me. I no longer go into instant fight-or-flight when someone raises their voice at me or tries to give me a high-five. If I stayed in those reactions then my abuser would still be victorious over me. I would still be his victim. I refuse! I refuse to allow him to dictate who I am or how I live life in any way. He had all of me he is going to get!

I can see now that those circumstances actually refined me and made me a better person. Prior to my abuse I viewed victims of violence in intimate relationships with some contempt. I saw them as "weak," lacking the strength or courage to leave their abuser. After being in that situation myself, my eyes were opened. I was not weak. But leaving was a tremendous risk to my life and the life of my child. It took years and many tries to get out of that situation alive. Experiencing that allowed me to have a deeper understanding of the complexity of abusive relationships. Because of that I now have much stronger empathy for others in similar situations, sharper survival instincts, and I am a person who can stand firm in who she is. I am a much better and more effective therapist because of the understanding and empathy I have gained from life experiences. What I experienced was not suffered in vain, it was for a greater purpose that I now see being played out daily. I love those parts of me, the parts honed and developed through trial, and today I can thank my abusers for helping to make me the person I am today.

I think this is most beautifully described by author Ann Voskamp in her book, "The Broken Way," in a poignant exchange between a mother and daughter:

"It's all okay." She finds the right first words. She holds the torn bit of her paper heart out to me. "Maybe the love gets in easier right where the heart's broke open?"

I blink at her, replaying the moment.

Maybe the love gets in easier right where the heart's broke open.

I pull her in close, gently kiss her in the middle of her perfect little forehead—and off she goes with her one broken heart. And I'd sat there in the wake of her, waking: maybe you can live a full and beautiful life in spite of the great and terrible moments that will happen right inside of you. Actually—maybe you get to become more abundant because of those moments. Maybe—I don't know how, but somehow?—maybe our hearts are made to be broken. Broken open. Broken free. Maybe the deepest wounds birth deepest wisdom (Voskamp 2016, pg 24).

Hmm…maybe the deepest wounds birth deepest wisdom. I'll trade my wounds in for wisdom. I'll trade my pain in for joy. I'll trade my weakness in for strength. And isn't that just exactly what is happening?

What about you? What are the things you want to overcome, to move past, to let go of? Can you accept that those things happened to you, but something good came of them? They no longer define you. You can lovingly embrace the person you are today BECAUSE of those things, rather than trying to cut those things off from who you are. Can you do that?? You're worth it!

"Eventually you will come to understand that love heals everything and love is all there is." -Gary Zukav

Chapter Twelve:
Moving Forward with
Hope....

Where do you go from here? I can tell you, I know what it feels like to be hopeless. To long for death to come because the life you face each day is just unbearable. To have no hope for change. Once I removed myself from the abuse, though, my hope began growing exponentially! Life is wonderful, if for no other reason than I don't have fear of being attacked in my bed in my sleep, I don't have fear of getting yelled at every night over dinner, and I know no one is coming to kick me out of my own house in the middle of the night (yes, all of those are things I experienced on a regular basis). I have peace in my own home now. And it is AMAZING!!!!

Imagine a world where you don't have to live in constant fear of being hurt. Where you can choose to be who you want to and do what you want to without repercussion. Where someone else is not constantly dictating your every move. Where you don't have to experience physical pain at the hands of someone you love. Imagine it, because it exists!! And you can travel there whenever you are ready. It awaits your presence with delight.

When I left my marriage I had no intention of dating or ever being in another relationship. The excruciating pain of loving an abusive narcissist had nearly cured me of any desire to couple again. I focused on surviving, healing, and finding joy in a simple life for me and my children. And it was Heaven! After a while, though, I started to entertain a relationship again. What if there was a man out there somewhere who wouldn't abuse me? What if there was someone who could accept and love me, flaws and all? What if....

Let's look for a moment at the facts:

- 1 in 4 women in the United States report experiencing violence at the hands of an intimate partner at some point in her life (*Centers for Disease Control and Prevention 2008*).

- 1 in 4 women and 1 in 7 men will experience severe physical violence by an intimate partner in their lifetime. (CDC, 2017)
- 1 in 10 women in the United States will be raped by an intimate partner in her lifetime. (CDC, 2010)
- Approximately 16.9% of women and 8.0% of men will experience sexual violence other than rape by an intimate partner at some point in their lifetime. (CDC, 2010)
- Nearly 1 in 3 women experience domestic violence in their lifetime.
  American Psychological Association Violence and the Family: Report of the American Psychological Association Presidential Task Force on Violence and the Family (1996, p 10).

Every nine seconds, a woman in America is assaulted or beaten, according to the <u>National Coalition Against Domestic Violence</u>. A mind-boggling one in three women (and one in four men) has been a victim of physical brutality by an intimate partner, the group also reports.

So, if the statistics say one in three women are involved in an abusive relationship at some point in their lifetime, then that means that: 1. you are not alone, and 2. two out of three women are in healthy non-abusive relationships for most of their lives. If two out of three women can find a healthy, safe partner, then why can't we? Why can't we join that upper percentile rank and enter into healthy relationships? The fact of the matter is that we can. If we heal our wounds and address our own unhealthy relationship patterns, then we are quite capable of learning how to avoid abusive personalities and find someone who is loving, supportive, and safe to partner with. Let that give you hope, not just for a better life, but for love if that is what you seek. If you choose to live a life free of fear, anxiety, and PTSD symptoms, but are happy and content in solitude, then give yourself permission for that, as well. The most important thing is that you heal, become whole, and find happiness. THAT is what life is all about!!

"Life isn't about waiting for the storm to pass...it's about learning to dance in the rain."

-Vivian Greene

Helpful Resources

Signs of a Trauma History

You may be wondering…..how do I know if I have experienced life-changing trauma in my past?? If I have no memory of it, how might it be affecting me? Or perhaps you are a clinician, wondering how to spot survivors among your clientele…how do I know if my client experienced childhood sexual abuse, perhaps has repressed memories, or has a complex trauma history? Here are a few of the "signs" you can look for. Keep in mind this is not an exhaustive list, there are other possible indicators I won't mention here, and you need not have all of these for this to apply. Also, the presence of these signs does not guarantee that you experienced trauma. Many factors are involved, but if you suspect trauma or abuse, the presence of these signs would indicate the possibility should be explored and considered. Keep in mind trauma includes witnessing abuse, accidents, death, and can include many things that do not involve you personally being harmed. Seek professional assistance if you find you have a number of these indicators before making assumptions that you have no evidence to support. Be careful with past memories…they are fragile and can be altered easily. Find someone who is experienced to help you on your discovery journey.

Physical Signs of Trauma:

- Unexplained sensations including pain
- Sleep and eating disturbances
- Low energy
- Increased arousal/hypervigilance
- Flight/Fight/Freeze

Emotional Symptoms:

- Depression and fear
- Struggles with emotional regulation
- Anxiety and panic
- Numbness, irritability, anger
- Feeling out of control
- Avoidance
- Inability to tolerate intense feelings
- Internal belief of being bad/worthless, or self-blame
- Attachment difficulties/disorganized attachment patterns

Cognitive:

- Distraction

- Decrease in concentration

- Memory lapse

- Difficulty with decisions

- Black and white thinking

- Learning difficulties

Behavioral Signs & Effects:

- Compulsion

- Substance abuse

- Eating disorders/food related issues

- Impulsive, self-destructive behavior

- Dissociation/Changes in interpersonal relationships:

- Isolation, avoidance, social withdrawal

- Sexual disruption

- Feeling threatened, hostile, argumentative

- Addictive behaviors

- Self-harming

- Developmental regression

- OCD/ticks

- Suicidality

Re-experiencing the trauma:

- Flashbacks

- Nightmares

- Intrusive thoughts

- Sudden emotional and or physical flooding

- Co-occurring Disorders

Trauma Symptom Checklist – 40

(Briere & Runtz, 1989)

How often have you experienced each of the following in the last month? Please choose one number, 0-4.

Symptom	Never---------------------Often				
	0	1	2	3	4
1. Headaches					
2. Insomnia					
3. Weight loss (w/o dieting)					
4. Stomach problems					
5. Sexual problems					
6. Feeling isolated from others					
7. "Flashbacks"					
8. Restless Sleep					
9. Low sex drive					
10. Anxiety attacks					
11. Sexual overactivity					
12. Loneliness					
13. Nightmares					
14. "Spacing out"					
15. Sadness					
16. Dizziness					
17. Feeling unsatisfied sexually					
18. Trouble controlling temper					
19. Waking up early in morning					
20. Uncontrollable crying					
21. Fear of men					
22. Not feeling rested in morning					
23. Having sex you didn't enjoy					
24. Trouble getting along with					
25. Memory problems					
26. Desire to physically hurt self					
27. Fear of women					
28. Waking up in the night					

Trauma Symptom Checklist Cont. – 40

(Briere & Runtz, 1989)

How often have you experienced each of the following in the last month? Please choose one number, 0-4.

Symptom	Never------------------------Often				
	0	1	2	3	4
29. Bad thghts/feelings during sex					
30. Passing out					
31.Feeling things are unreal					
32. Unnecessary washing					
33.Feelings of inferiority					
34.Feeling tense all the time					
35. Confusion about sxual feelngs					
36.Desire to physically hurt othrs					
37.Feelings of guilt					
38.Feeling of being out of body					
39. Having trouble breathing					
40.Sxual feelings when shouldn't					

Trauma Symptom Checklist – 40 (Briere & Runtz, 1989)

Subscale composition and scoring for the TSC-40: The score for each subscale is the sum of the relevant items.

Dissociation – 7, 14, 16, 25, 31, 38

Anxiety – 1, 4, 10, 16, 21, 27, 32, 34, 39

Depression – 2, 3, 9, 15, 19, 20, 26, 33, 37

SATI (Sexual Abuse Trauma Index) – 5, 7, 13, 21, 25, 29, 31

Sleep Disturbance – 2, 8, 13, 19, 22, 28

Sexual Problems – 5, 9, 11, 17, 23, 29, 35, 40

TSC Total Score: 1-40

Important Note: This measure assesses trauma-related problems in several categories. According to John Briere, PhD "The TSC-40 is a research instrument only. Use of this scale is limited to professional researchers. It is not intended as, nor should it be used as, a self-test under any circumstances." For a more current version of the measure, which can be used for clinical purposes (and for which there is a fee), consider the Trauma Symptom Inventory – contact Psychological Assessment Resources at 800-331-8378. The TSC-40 is freely available to researchers. No additional permission is required for use or reproduction of this measure, although the following citation is needed: Briere, J.N. & Runtz, M.G. (1989). The Trauma Symptom Checklist (TSC-33): Early data on a new scale. Journal of Interpersonal Violence, 4, 151-163. For further information on the measure, go to www.johnbriere.com.

*This checklist is not intended for self-diagnostic purposes but rather to give you an idea of some of the symptoms associated through research with PTSD and a history of trauma. On the following page you will find a self-assessment that can be an indicator of a possible PTSD diagnosis. If your score is 33 or higher, you are at risk for PTSD. Having a professional assessment done would be suggested as self-assessments cannot accurately diagnose.

(Obtained from the National Center for PTSD)

PTSD Checklist (PCL) - 5

Name:_____   Date:_____

Instructions: Below is a list of problems that people sometimes have in response to a very stressful experience. Please read each problem carefully and then circle one of the numbers to the right to indicate how much you have been bothered by that problem <u>in the past month.</u>

In the past month, how much were you bothered by:	Not at all	A little bit	Moderately	Quite a bit	Extremely
1. Repeated, disturbing, and unwanted memories of the stressful experience?	0	1	2	3	4
2. Repeated, disturbing dreams of the stressful experience?	0	1	2	3	4
3. Suddenly feeling or acting as if the stressful experience were actually happening again (as if you were actually back there reliving it)?	0	1	2	3	4
4. Feeling very upset when something reminded you of the stressful experience?	0	1	2	3	4
5. Having strong physical reactions when something reminded you of the stressful experience (for example, heart pounding, trouble breathing, sweating)?	0	1	2	3	4
6. Avoiding memories, thoughts, or feelings related to the stressful experience?	0	1	2	3	4
7. Avoiding external reminders of the stressful experience (for example, people, places, conversations, activities, objects, or situations)?	0	1	2	3	4
8. Trouble remembering important parts of the stressful experience?	0	1	2	3	4
9. Having strong negative beliefs about yourself, other people, or the world (for example, having thoughts such as: I am bad, there is something seriously wrong with me, no one can be trusted, the world is completely dangerous)?	0	1	2	3	4
10. Blaming yourself or someone else for the stressful experience or what happened after it?	0	1	2	3	4
11. Having strong negative feelings such as fear, horror, anger, guilt, or shame?	0	1	2	3	4
12. Loss of interest in activities that you used to enjoy?	0	1	2	3	4
13. Feeling distant or cut off from other people?	0	1	2	3	4
14. Trouble experiencing positive feelings (for example, being unable to feel happiness or have loving feelings for people close to you)?	0	1	2	3	4
15. Irritable behavior, angry outbursts, or acting aggressively?	0	1	2	3	4
16. Taking too many risks or doing things that could cause you harm?	0	1	2	3	4
17. Being "superalert" or watchful or on guard?	0	1	2	3	4
18. Feeling jumpy or easily startled?	0	1	2	3	4
19. Having difficulty concentrating?	0	1	2	3	4
20. Trouble falling or staying asleep?	0	1	2	3	4

DSM-5 Criteria For a PTSD Dx:

How do you know if you have PTSD, C-PTSD, or suffer from a trauma-related disorder? Do your research, first of all. I am always a proponent of clients/patients being their own advocates and educating themselves. If you have particular "symptoms" that are hindering your functionality, investigate what possible disorders those symptoms correlate with. Keep in mind that you can have symptoms of many disorders and not actually have any disorder. According to the standard, you must meet all required criteria to be officially diagnosed with a disorder. Also keep in mind that each person is a unique individual and how any particular disorder affects you may differ from the "norm" or standard. Rest assured that with appropriate treatment most disorders can be overcome to go on and live a happy, productive life. The point of this book, in fact, is to help you be your best self DESPITE any potential diagnosis you may have. For the purposes of determining if this book applies to you and may be helpful, I am listing the diagnostic criteria for PTSD (must also be met for C-PTSD) below:

Full criteria are available from the American Psychiatric Association. All of the criteria are required for a diagnosis of PTSD. Below is a summary of the diagnostic criteria:

Criterion A (one required): The person was exposed to: death, threatened death, actual or threatened serious injury, or actual or threatened sexual violence, in the following way(s):

- Direct exposure
- Witnessing the trauma
- Learning that a relative or close friend was exposed to a trauma
- Indirect exposure to aversive details of the trauma, usually in the course of professional duties (e.g., first responders, medics)

Criterion B (one required): The traumatic event is persistently re-experienced, in the following way(s):

- Unwanted upsetting memories
- Nightmares
- Flashbacks
- Emotional distress after exposure to traumatic reminders
- Physical reactivity after exposure to traumatic reminders

Criterion C (one required): Avoidance of trauma-related stimuli after the trauma, in the following way(s):

- Trauma-related thoughts or feelings
- Trauma-related reminders

Criterion D (two required): Negative thoughts or feelings that began or worsened after the trauma, in the following way(s):

- Inability to recall key features of the trauma
- Overly negative thoughts and assumptions about oneself or the world
- Exaggerated blame of self or others for causing the trauma
- Negative affect
- Decreased interest in activities
- Feeling isolated
- Difficulty experiencing positive affect

Criterion E (two required): Trauma-related arousal and reactivity that began or worsened after the trauma, in the following way(s):

- Irritability or aggression
- Risky or destructive behavior
- Hypervigilance
- Heightened startle reaction
- Difficulty concentrating
- Difficulty sleeping

Criterion F (required): Symptoms last for more than 1 month.

Criterion G (required): Symptoms create distress or functional impairment (e.g., social, occupational).

Criterion H (required): Symptoms are not due to medication, substance use, or other illness.

Two specifications:

- **<u>Dissociative Specification</u>.** In addition to meeting criteria for diagnosis, an individual experiences high levels of either of the following in reaction to trauma-related stimuli:
  - Depersonalization. Experience of being an outside observer of or detached from oneself (e.g., feeling as if "this is not happening to me" or one were in a dream).
  - Derealization. Experience of unreality, distance, or distortion (e.g., "things are not real").
- **Delayed Specification.** Full diagnostic criteria are not met until at least six months after the trauma(s), although onset of symptoms may occur immediately.

Note: *DSM-5* introduced a preschool subtype of PTSD for children ages six years and younger.

<u>What is the difference between the previous DSM criteria and the new DSM-5 criteria for PTSD:</u>

Overall, the symptoms of PTSD are generally comparable between *DSM-5* and *DSM-IV*. A few key alterations include:

- The revision of Criterion A1 in *DSM-5* narrowed qualifying traumatic events such that the unexpected death of family or a close friend due to natural causes is no longer included.
- Criterion A2, requiring that the response to a traumatic event involved intense fear, hopelessness, or horror, was removed

from *DSM-5*. Research suggests that Criterion A2 did not improve diagnostic accuracy (2).
- The avoidance and numbing cluster (Criterion C) in *DSM-IV* was separated into two criteria in *DSM-5*: Criterion C (avoidance) and Criterion D (negative alterations in cognitions and mood). This results in a requirement that a PTSD diagnosis includes at least one avoidance symptom.
- Three new symptoms were added:
  - Criterion D (Negative thoughts or feelings that began or worsened after the trauma): Overly negative thoughts and assumptions about oneself or the world; and, negative affect
  - Criterion E (Trauma-related arousal and reactivity that began or worsened after the trauma): Reckless or destructive behavior

Effective Clinical Modalities for PTSD/Trauma-Related Issues:

Introduction

Here I will discuss this most widely used and accepted treatment modalities for trauma and PTSD. I will briefly describe each modality and then discuss the effectiveness of each, based on current research studies. The most common treatment models at this time are:

- **Prolonged-exposure therapy:** PE therapy was developed for use with PTSD by Terence Keane, University of Pennsylvania psychologist Edna Foa, PhD, and Emory University psychologist Barbara O. Rothbaum, PhD. In this modality of treatment, a therapist guides the client to recall traumatic memories in a controlled fashion so that clients eventually regain mastery of their thoughts and feelings around the incident. While exposing people to the very events that caused their trauma may seem counterintuitive, Rothbaum emphasizes that it's done in a gradual, controlled and repeated manner, until the person can evaluate their circumstances realistically and understand they can safely return to the activities in their current lives that they had been avoiding.

- **Cognitive-processing therapy:** CPT is a form of cognitive behavioral therapy, or CBT, developed by Boston University psychologist Patricia A. Resick, PhD, director of the women's health sciences division of the National Center for PTSD, specifically to treat victims of rape. This treatment was later used with PTSD and is now one of the more commonly accepted models for PTSD. This treatment includes an exposure component but places greater emphasis on cognitive strategies to help people alter faulty thinking or belief systems that have emerged because of the traumatic event. Practitioners may work with clients on false beliefs that the world is no longer safe, for example, or that they are incompetent because they have "let" a terrible event happen to them.

- **Stress-inoculation training**: Stress-inoculation training is another form of CBT, where practitioners teach clients techniques to manage and reduce anxiety, such as breathing, muscle relaxation and positive self-talk.

- **Other forms of cognitive therapy:** Other forms of cognitive therapy, including cognitive restructuring, are also used to treat PTSD.

- **Eye-movement desensitization and reprocessing**: EMDR, developed by Francine Shapiro, a psychologist from the Mental Research Institute, is a model of therapy involving guided eye movements or tapping while activating the limbic area of the brain. Brain scans show evidence that this form of therapy does activate and relocated traumatic memories within the brain and reduce PTSD symptoms dramatically. EMDR requires specific training and cannot be done by a therapist who is not educated and trained in the EMDR model.

- **Medications:** Selective serotonin reuptake inhibitors are the most common medication used to treat PTSD. Two in particular-paroxetine (Paxil) and sertraline (Zoloft)-have been approved by the Food and Drug Administration for use with PTSD. Other medications may be useful in treating PTSD as well, particularly when the person has additional disorders such as depression, anxiety or psychosis, the guidelines note. However, medication is meant to alleviate the symptoms while addressing the root issues in therapy. Medication is not intended to nor is it effective in resolving the PTSD altogether.

Discussion

There are several prominent Clinical Practice Guidelines clinicians can access and use to inform their treatment of clients/patients with traumatic issues, including PTSD and C-PTSD. These guidelines are set by experts in the field based on the most recent research studies on treatment modalities for trauma-related issues. One such guideline, widely accepted and used professionally, is the VA/DoD PTSD Clinical Practice Guideline (CPG) for Posttraumatic Stress Disorder (2017). This CPG gives evidence-based recommendations for the treatment of PTSD, including individual trauma-focused psychotherapy, Prolonged Exposure (PE), Cognitive Processing Therapy (CPT), and Eye Movement Desensitization and Reprocessing (EMDR), which are listed as the most effective treatments for PTSD (Department of Veterans Affairs and Department of Defense 2017).

Individual trauma-focused psychotherapy (PE, CPT, EMDR) is recommended by the CPG (2017) above medication based on recent research. The results of two recent meta-analyses which compared the treatment effects of psychotherapy with pharmacotherapy showed that trauma-focused psychotherapy leads to greater improvement in PTSD symptoms than medication, furthermore, those improvements last longer (Lee, Schnitzlein, et al. 2016, and Watts, Schnurr, et al. 2013). This doesn't take into account the risk for negative side effects which are generally greater with medication than psychotherapy (one potential side effect of medication often being suicide) (Department of Veterans Affairs and Department of Defense 2017).

Trauma-focused psychotherapy is defined by the CPG (2017) as therapy that uses cognitive, emotional, or behavioral techniques to facilitate processing a traumatic event or memory, in which the trauma is a central focus of the therapeutic process. The psychotherapy models which have the strongest evidence from clinical studies are PE (Foa, Hembree, et al 2005), CPT (Resick, Nishith, et al 2002), and EMDR (Shapiro 1989, and Rothbaum, Astin et al 2005). These models have been tested in numerous clinical trials with long-term follow up designs in patients with complex co-morbidities and were validated by research teams not involved with the development of the treatment models (Department of Veterans Affairs and Department of Defense 2017). Other models that have enough evidence to warrant recommendation are: specific cognitive behavioral therapies for PTSD (Ehlers, Hackmann, et al 2003; Ehlers, Grey et al 2013; Ehlers, Grey et al 2014, Blanchard, Hickling et al 2003; Bryant et al 2008), Brief Eclectic Therapy (Gersons, Carlier et al 2000), Narrative Exposure Therapy (Ertl, Pfieffer, et al 2011), and written narrative exposure (Resick, Galovski, et al 2008). There are other psychotherapy models, however, no other model is backed by research at this time (Department of Veterans Affairs and Department of Defense 2017).

Exposure-based treatments have been the focus of the greatest number of studies, with PE being the most prevalent. In studies comparing present-centered therapy with PE, participants with PTSD diagnostic criteria and who received the PE modality experienced a greater reduction of PTSD symptoms (Foa, Rothbaum, et al 1998). CPT is one of the most well-researched cognitive models and has also been demonstrated via studies to produce more and faster improvement than a control group (Watts, Schnurr, et al 2013). EMDR has also shown effectiveness in research for more significant, faster, and long-term improvement in reduction of PTSD symptoms (find a research study). Overall, CPT, PE, and EMDR have shown remarkable success in outcome research, but it is still uncertain if one modality is "better" than another. In research comparing the effectiveness of PE versus EMDR, one study found equal results (Rothbaum, Astin et al 2005), while another found PE to be superior (Taylor, Thordarson, et al. 2003).

There is also evidence to support the effectiveness of the use of writing therapeutically. Written narrative exposure therapies focus on writing about the traumatic memory, often having the patient write their account and review their writing with the therapist, then rereading it for homework (Resick, Galovski, et al. 2008). Written narrative exposure therapies (WET) have also been shown effective as stand-alone treatment for PTSD (Resick, Galovski, et al. 2008). Other treatment modalities may also be effective, at this time, though there is not sufficient evidence to present an opinion as to the effectiveness of any other models. More research is needed to demonstrate the effectiveness of the wide variety of models available.

Conclusion

Individual trauma-focused psychotherapies are the most recommended, research-based treatments for PTSD, the most prevalent of those including PE, CPT, and EMDR (Department of Veterans Affairs and Department of Defense 2017). Specific medications and other interventions can help reduce the symptoms of PTSD, but more research is needed before drawing conclusions about the effectiveness of other psychotherapies.

Resources for HELP

- **<u>CALL 911</u> if you are in immediate danger of harming yourself, being harmed by someone else, or harming others!!!!**
- **Your local, toll-free state 24-hr CRISIS line will have counselors available and can refer you to the best resources for your situation**
- **National Suicide Prevention Lifeline Number: 1-800-273-TALK (8255)**
- **Georgia Crisis and Access Line (GCAL): 1-800-715-4225**
- **Crisis Text Line: Text NAMI to 741-741**
- **National Domestic Violence Hotline: 1-800-799-SAFE (7233)**
- **National Domestic Violence Chat online at <u>www.thehotline.org</u>**
- **National Sexual Assault Hotline: 1-800-656-HOPE (4673)**
- **1-800-4-A-CHILD (1-800-422-4453): Crisis Counseling for Children or Adult Survivors.**
- **RAINN: 1-800-656-HOPE (4673) for National Sexual Assault Hotline.**
- **NAMI: 1-800-950-NAMI (6264) or <u>info@nami.org</u>**

* The NAMI HelpLine can be reached M-F 10 am to 6 pm ET.

**National Center for PTSD: www.ptsd.va.gov

**See suggested coping mechanisms on the back of this page if this is not an emergency situation

WAYS TO COPE WHEN STRUGGLING

Things you can use to get through the moment

- Exercise   * Running, Walking, Yoga, Dance
- Art   *Painting, Sculpting, Drawing, Photography
- Writing   *Journaling, Poetry, Songs, Letters
- Reading
- Television/Movies
- Music
- Cleaning
- Hot/Cold Shower or Bath
- Call someone close to you
- Go visit a friend or family member
- Take a nap
- Meditation
- Guided visualization
- Find something funny to watch or read
- Crochet or knit
- Do something creative
- Pray
- Call a crisis line to speak with a counselor
- Allow yourself to feel the emotions
- FIVE SENSES: use taste, touch, sound, smell, and sight to ground you or calm you (example: a comforting texture or scent, or a photograph of a loved one; the sound of a waterfall or an uplifting song)
- SENSATIONS-if experiencing an extreme emotion, use a sensation to "shock" you out of that emotion. i.e. Really cold shower, loud music for a second, a really hot bath, a sharp or spicy taste, holding ice in your hand until it melts, snapping a rubber band on your wrist

(Taken from the DBT skillsets developed by M. Linehan)

Resources on Trauma

References and Recommended Reading

American Psychiatric Association. *Diagnostic and statistical manual of mental disorders, (5ᵗʰ ed.),* Washington, DC: Author, 2013.

American Psychiatric Association (2004). *Practice Guideline for the Treatment of Patients with Acute Stress Disorder and Posttraumatic Stress Disorder.* Arlington, VA: American Psychiatric Association Practice Guidelines.

American Psychological Association. *Violence and the Family: Report of the American Psychological Association Presidential Task Force on Violence and the Family,* 1996.

Barry, Michael, Dr. *The Forgiveness Project: The Startling Discovery of How to Overcome Cancer, Find Health, and Achieve Peace,* 2010.

Black, M.C., Basile, K.C., Breiding, M.J., Smith, S.G., Walters, M.L., Merrick, M.T., Chen, J. & Stevens, M. (2011). *The national intimate partner and sexual violence survey: 2010 summary report.* Retrieved from http://www.cdc.gov/violenceprevention/pdf/nisvs_report2010-a.pdf.

Blevins, C.A., Weathers, F.W., et al. *The Posttraumatic Stress Disorder Checklist for DSM-5 (PCL-5): Development and initial psychometric evaluation.* Journal of Traumatic Stress, 28, 489-498, 2015.

Briere, J.N., & Runtz, M.G. (1989). The Trauma Symptom Checklist (TSC-33): early data on a new scale. *Journal of Interpersonal Violence, 4,* 151-163.

Brown, Brené. *Braving the Wilderness: The Quest for True Belonging and the Courage to Stand Alone.* Random House Publishing, 2017.

Brown, Brené. *Daring Greatly: How the Courage to Be Vulnerable Transforms the Way We Live, Love, Parent, and Lead.* New York City, NY: Gotham, 2012.

Brown, Brené. *Rising Strong: The Reckoning, The Rumble, The Revolution.* Random House Publishing, 2015.

Center for Disease Control and Prevention. *National Intimate Partner and Sexual Violence Survey. Retrieved from:* https://www.cdc.gov/violenceprevention/pdf/nisvs_executive_summary-a.pdf

Consumer Reports. "*Eat Smarter, Eat Healthier.*" September 2017. Retrieved from: https://www.consumerreports.org/healthy-eating/eat-smarter-eat-healthier-sugar-salt-fat-gluten/

Courtois, C. A., and Ford, J. D., eds. *Treating Complex Traumatic Stress Disorders: An Evidence-Based Guide.* Foreword by J. L. Herman. Afterward by B. A. van der Kolk. New York: Guilford Press, 2009.

Department of Veterans Affairs and Department of Defense. *VA/DOD Clinical Practice Guideline for the Management of Posttraumatic Stress Disorder and Acute Stress Disorder.* Washington DC, 2017. Retrieved from: https://www.healthquality.va.gov/guidelines/MH/ptsd/

Ehrmann, Max. "Desiderata*." The Poems of Max Ehrmann.* Bruce Humphries, Inc, 1948.

Enright, R.D. 2001. *Forgiveness is a choice: A step-by-step process for resolving anger and restoring hope.* Washington, DC: APA Life Tools.

Foa, E.B., Keane, T.M., Friedman, M.J., & Cohen, J.A. (2009). *Effective treatments for PTSD: Practice Guidelines of the International Society for Traumatic Stress Studies* New York: Guilford Press.

Forgiveness Steps. (n.d.). Retrieved from http://learningtoforgive.com/9-steps/

Greater Good. 2004. Retrieved from: https://greatergood.berkeley.edu/article/item/nine_steps_to_forgiveness

Harris WS, Gowda M, Kolb JW, et al. A Randomized, Controlled Trial of the Effects of Remote, Intercessory Prayer on Outcomes in Patients Admitted to the Coronary Care Unit. *Arch Intern Med.* 1999;159(19):2273–2278. doi:10.1001/archinte.159.19.2273

Johnson, Lorie. "The Deadly Consequences of Forgiveness." June 2015. CBN News, Retrieved from:

http://www1.cbn.com/cbnnews/healthscience/2015/june/the-deadly-consequences-of-unforgiveness

Kennard, Deborah. EMDR Basic Training S.A.F.E. Approach. Personal Transformation Institute, 2015.

Koenig, Harold, McCullough, Michael, & Larson, David. *The Handbook of Religion and Health,* New York, NY:Oxford University Press, 2011.

Miller, L., Bansal, R., et al. *Neuroanatomical Correlates of Religiosity and Spirituality.* JAMA Psychiatry, 2013;1 DOI:10, 1001/hamapsychiatry.2013.3067

Miller, L., Wickramaratne, P., Tenke, C., Weissman, M. (2012). *Spirituality and Major Depression: A Ten-Year Prospective Study, American Journal of Psychiatry,* 169 (1), 89-94.

National Coalition Against Domestic Violence. https://ncadv.org/statistics.

https://www.speakcdn.com/assets/2497/domestic_violence.pdf

National Center for PTSD, VA Medical Center. White River Junction, VT, 2015.

National Center for PTSD. *PTSD Research Quarterly: Advancing Science and Promoting Understanding of Traumatic Stress,* Vol. 26(4).

Newsmax Health. "Science Proves the Healing Power of Prayer ." March 31, 2015, Retrieved from:

https://www.newsmax.com/health/headline/prayer-health-faith-medicine/2015/03/31/id/635623/

Norman, Kathi. "Forgiveness: How it Manifests in Our Health, Wellbeing, and Longetivity." Scholarly Commons, University of Pennsylvania, August 2017.

Ogrodnick, L. (2008). *Family Violence in Canada: A Statistical Profile 2008.* Ottawa: Statistics Canada

Oksana, Chrystine, *Safe Passage to Healing: A Guide for Survivors of Ritual Abuse.* HarperPerennial. Lincoln, NE, 2001.

Rosenbloom, Dena, Williams, Marybeth, & Watkins, Barbara. *Life After Trauma, 2nd ed, A Workbook for Healing.* Guilford Press, NY, 2010.

Schwartz, Karen. Schwartz, Karen, *Forgiveness: How Letting Go of Grudges is Good for Your Health*. John Hopkins Health, Summer 2014.

Shapiro, Francine. *Eye Movement Desensitization and Reprocessing [EMDR] Therapy, 3rd ed.: Basic Principles, Protocols, and Procedures*. New York, The Guilford Press, 2018.

Standiford, Steve, *Cancer Treatment Center of America*, Philiadelphia, PA, 2015.

U.S. Department of Veterans Affairs. PTSD: National Center for PTSD. Retrieved from http://www.ptsd.va.gov/professional/assessment/adult-sr/ptsd-checklist.asp. 2016.

Van der Kolk, B.A., ed. *Post-traumatic Stress Disorder: Psychological and Biological Sequelae*. Washington DC:American Psychiatric Press, 1984.

Van der Kolk, B.A., *Psychological Trauma*. Washington DC, American Psychiatric Press, 1987.

Van der Kolk, B.A. *The Body Keeps the Score: Brain, Mind, and Body in the Healing of Trauma*. Viking Press, 2014.

Van der Kolk, B.A., McFarlane AC, Weisaeth L (editors): *Traumatic Stress: the effects of overwhelming experience on mind, body and society*. New York, Guilford Press, 1996.

Voskamp, Ann. *The Broken Way: a daring path into the abundant life*. Zondervan, Michigan. 2016.

World Health Organization (2013). *Guidelines for the management of conditions that are specifically related to stress*. Geneva, WHO.

Research References for Clinical Modalities

Lee, D. J., Schnitzlein, C. W., Wolf, J. P., Vythilingam, M., Rasmusson, A. M., & Hoge, C. W. (2016). Psychotherapy versus pharmacotherapy for posttraumatic stress disorder: Systematic review and meta-analyses to determine first-line treatments. *Depression and Anxiety, 33*, 792-806. doi:10.1002/da.22511

Watts, B. V., Schnurr, P. P., Mayo, L., Young-Xu, Y., Weeks, W. B., & Friedman, M. J. (2013). Meta-analysis of the efficacy of treatments for posttraumatic stress disorder. *Journal of Clinical Psychiatry, 74*, e541-550. doi:10.4088/JCP.12r08225

Schnurr, P. P. (2017). Focusing on trauma-focused psychotherapy for posttraumatic stress disorder. *Current Opinion in Psychology, 14*, 56-60. doi:10.1016/j.copsych.2016.11.005

Foa, E. B., Hembree, E. A., Cahill, S. P., Rauch, S. A. M., Riggs, D. S., Feeny, N. C., & Yadin, E. (2005). Randomized trial of Prolonged Exposure for posttraumatic stress disorder with and without cognitive restructuring: Outcome at academic and community clinics. *Journal of Consulting and Clinical Psychology, 73*, 953-964. doi:10.1037/0022-006X.73.5.953

Resick, P. A., Nishith, P., Weaver, T. L., Astin, M. C., & Feuer, C. A. (2002). A comparison of Cognitive Processing Therapy with Prolonged Exposure and a waiting condition for the treatment of chronic posttraumatic stress disorder in female rape victims. *Journal of Consulting and Clinical Psychology, 70*, 867-879. doi:10.1037/0022-006X.70.4.867

Shapiro, F. (1989). Eye movement desensitization: A new treatment for post-traumatic stress disorder. *Journal of Behavior Therapy and Experimental Psychiatry, 20*, 211-217. doi:10.1016/0005-7916(89)90025-6

Rothbaum, B. O., Astin, M. C., & Marstellar, F. (2005). Prolonged Exposure versus Eye Movement Desensitization and Reprocessing (EMDR) for PTSD rape victims. *Journal of Traumatic Stress, 18*, 607-616. doi:10.1002/jts.20069

Ehlers, A., Clark, D. M., Hackmann, A., McManus, F., Fennell, M., Herbert, C., & Mayou, R. (2003). A randomized controlled trial of cognitive therapy, a self-help booklet, and repeated assessments as early interventions for posttraumatic stress disorder. *Archives of General Psychiatry, 60*, 1024-1032. doi:10.1001/archpsyc.60.10.1024

Ehlers, A., Grey, N., Wild, J., Stott, R., Liness, S., Deale, A., Handley, R., Albert, I. Cullen, D., Hackmann, A., Manley, J., McManus, F., Brady, F., Salkovskis, P., & Clark, D. M. (2013). Implementation of cognitive therapy for PTSD in routine clinical care: Effectiveness and moderators of outcome in a consecutive sample. *Behaviour Research and Therapy, 51,* 742-752. doi:10.1016/j.brat.2013.08.006

Ehlers, A., Hackmann, A., Grey, N., Wild, J., Liness, S., Albert, I., Deale, A., Scott, R., & Clark, D. M. (2014). A randomized controlled trial of 7-day intensive and standard weekly cognitive therapy for PTSD and emotion-focused supportive therapy. *American Journal of Psychiatry, 171,* 294-304. doi:10.1176/appi.ajp.2013.12040552

Blanchard, E. B., Hickling, E. J., Devineni, T., Veazey, C. H., Galovski, T. E., Mundy, E., Malta, L. S. & Buckley, T. C. (2003). A controlled evaluation of cognitive behavioral therapy for posttraumatic stress in motor vehicle accident survivors. *Behaviour Research and Therapy, 41,* 79-96. doi:10.1016/S0005-7967(01)00131-0

Bryant, R. A., Mastrodomenico, J., Felmingham, K. L., Hopwood, S., Kenny, L., Kandris, E., Cahill, C., & Creamer, M. (2008). Treatment of acute stress disorder: A randomized controlled trial. *Archives of General Psychiatry, 65,*659-667. doi:10.1001/archpsych.65.6.659

Bryant, R. A., Moulds, M. L., Guthrie, R. M., Dang, S. T., Mastrodomenico, J., Nizon, R. D. V., Felmingham, K. L., Hopwood, S., & Creamer, M. (2008). A randomized controlled trial of exposure therapy and cognitive restructuring for posttraumatic stress disorder. *Journal of Consulting and Clinical Psychology, 76,* 695-703. doi:10.1037/a0012616

Kubany, E. S., Hill, E. E., Owens, J. A., Iannce-Spencer, C., McCaig, M. A., Tremayne, K. J., & WIlliams, P. L. (2004). Cognitive trauma therapy for battered women with PTSD (CTT-BW). *Journal of Consulting and Clinical Psychology, 72,* 3-18. doi:10.1037/0022-006X.72.1.3

Marks, I., Lovell, K., Noshirvani, H., Livanou, M., & Thrasher, S. (1998). Treatment of posttraumatic stress disorder by exposure and/or cognitive restructuring: A controlled study. *Archives of General Psychiatry, 55,* 317-325. doi:10.1001/archpsyc.55.4.317

Power, K., McGoldrick, T., Brown, K., Buchanan, R., Sharp, D., Swanson, V., & Karatzias, A. (2002). A controlled comparison of eye movement desensitization and reprocessing versus exposure plus cognitive restructuring versus waiting list in the treatment of postâ€• traumatic stress disorder. *Clinical Psychology & Psychotherapy, 9,* 299-318. doi:10.1002/cpp.341

Gersons, B. P., Carlier, I. V., Lamberts, R. D., van der Kolk, B. A. (2000). Randomized clinical trial of brief eclectic psychotherapy for police officers with posttraumatic stress disorder. *Journal of Traumatic Stress, 13,* 333-347. doi:10.1023/A:1007793803627

Lindauer, R. J., Gersons, B. P., van Meijel, E. P., Blom, K., Carlier, I. V. E., Vrijlandt, I. & Olff, M. (2005). Effects of brief eclectic psychotherapy in patients with posttraumatic stress disorder: Randomized clinical trial. *Journal of Traumatic Stress, 18,* 205-212. doi:10.1002/jts.20029

Nijdam, M. J., Gersons, B. P., Reitsma, J. B., de Jongh, A., & Olff, M. (2012). Brief eclectic psychotherapy v. eye movement desensitization and reprocessing therapy for post-traumatic stress disorder: Randomized controlled trial. *British Journal of Psychiatry, 200,* 224-231. doi:10.1192/bjp.bp.111.099234

Erol, V., Pfeiffer, A., Schauer, E., Elbert, T., & Neuner, F. (2011). Community-implemented trauma therapy for former child soldiers in Northern Uganda: A randomized controlled trial. *Journal of the American Medical Association, 306,* 503-512. doi:10.1001/jama.2011.1060

Stembark, H., Catani, C., Neuner, F., Elbert, T., & Holen, A. Treating PTSD in refugees and asylum seekers within the general health care system. A randomized controlled multicenter study. *Behaviour Research and Therapy, 51,* 641-647. doi:10.1016/j.brat.2013.07.002

Resick, P. A., Galovski, T. E., Uhlmansiek, M. O., Scher, C. D., Clum, G. A., & Young-Xu, Y. (2008). A randomized clinical trial to dismantle components of Cognitive Processing Therapy for posttraumatic stress disorder in female victims of interpersonal violence. *Journal of Consulting and Clinical Psychology, 76,* 243-258. doi:10.1037/0022-006X.76.2.243

Sloan, D. M., Marx, B. P., Bovin, M. J., Feinstein, B. A., & Gallagher, M. W. (2012). Written exposure as an intervention for PTSD: A randomized clinical trial with motor vehicle accident survivors. *Behaviour Research and Therapy, 50,* 627-635. doi:10.1016/j.brat.2012.07.001

Sloan, D. M., Marx, B. P., Lee, D. J., & Resick, P. A. (2018). A brief exposure-based treatment vs Cognitive Processing Therapy for posttraumatic stress disorder: A randomized noninferiority clinical trial. *JAMA Psychiatry, Advance online publication.* doi:10.1001/jamapsychiatry.2017.4249

Foa, E. B., & Rothbaum, B. O. (1998). *Treating the trauma of rape: Cognitive behavioral therapy for PTSD* (1-266). New York, NY: Guilford.

Schnurr, P. P., Friedman, M. J., Engel, C. C., Foa, E. B., Shea, M. T., Chow, B. K., Resick, P. A., Thurston, V., Orsillo, S. M., Haug, R., Turner, C. & Bernardy, N. (2007). Cognitive behavioral therapy for posttraumatic stress disorder in women: A randomized controlled trial. *Journal of the American Medical Association, 297,* 820-830. doi:10.1001/jama.297.8.820

Foa, E. B., Dancu, C.V., Hembree, E. A., Jaycox, L.H., Meadows, E. A., & Street, G.P. (1999). A comparison of exposure therapy, Stress Inoculation Training, and their combination for reducing posttraumatic stress disorder in female assault victims. *Journal of Consulting and Clinical Psychology, 67,*194-200. doi:10.1037//0022-006X.67.2.194

Resick, P.A., & Schnicke, M. K. (1996). *Cognitive Processing Therapy for rape victims: A treatment manual.* Newbury Park, CA: Sage Publications.

Monson, C. M., Schnurr, P. P., Resick, P. A., Friedman, M. J., Young-Xu, Y., & Stevens, S. P. (2006). Cognitive Processing Therapy for Veterans with military-related posttraumatic stress disorder. *Journal of Consulting and Clinical Psychology, 74,* 898-907. doi:10.1037/0022-006X.74.5.898

Devilly, G. J. (2002). Eye Movement Desensitization and Reprocessing: A chronology of its development and scientific standing. *The Scientific Review of Mental Health Practice, 1,* 113-138.

Davidson, P. R., & Parker, K. C. H. (2001). Eye Movement Desensitization and Reprocessing (EMDR): A meta-analysis. *Journal of Consulting and Clinical Psychology, 69,* 305-316. doi:10.1037//0022-006X.69.2.305

Lee, C. W., & Cuijpers, P. (2013). A meta-analysis of the contribution of eye movements in processing emotional memories. *Journal of Behavior Therapy and Experimental Psychiatry, 44,* 231-239. doi:10.1016/j.jbtep.2012.11.001

Taylor, S., Thordarson, D. S., Maxfield, L., Fedoroff, I.C., Lovell, K., & Ogrodniczuk, J.S. (2003). Comparative efficacy, speed, and adverse effects of three PTSD treatments: Exposure therapy, EMDR, and relaxation training. *Journal of Consulting and Clinical Psychology, 71,* 330-338. doi:10.1037/0022-006X.71.2.330

Ehlers, A., & Clark, D. M. (2000). A cognitive model of posttraumatic stress disorder. *Behavioral Research and Therapy, 38,* 319-345. doi:10.1016/S0005-7967(99)00123-0

Duffy, M., Gillespie, K., & Clark, D. M. (2007). Post-traumatic stress disorder in the context of terrorism and other civil conflict in Northern Ireland: randomized controlled trial. *British Medical Journal, 334,* 1147-1150. doi:10.1136/bmj.39021.846852.BE

Bisson, J. I., Roberts N. P., Andrew, M., Cooper, R., & Lewis, K. (2013). Psychological therapies for chronic post-traumatic stress disorder (PTSD) in adults. *Cochrane Database of Systematic Reviews, 12.* Art. No.: CD003388. doi:10.1002/14651858.CD003388.pub4

Meichenbaum, D. H., & Deffenbacher, J. L. (1988). Stress Inoculation Training. *The Counseling Psychologist, 16,* 69-90. doi:10.1177/0011000088161005

Suris, A., Link-Malcolm, J., Chard, K., Ahn, C., & North, C. (2013). A randomized clinical trial of Cognitive Processing Therapy for Veterans with PTSD related to military sexual trauma. *Journal of Trauma Stress, 26,* 28-37. doi:10.1002/jts.21765

Markowitz, J. C., Petkova, E., Biyanova, T., Ding, K., Suh, E. J., & Neria, Y. (2015). Exploring personality diagnosis stability following acute psychotherapy for chronic posttraumatic stress disorder. *Depression and Anxiety, 32,* 919-926. doi:10.1002/da22436

Markowitz, J. C., Petkova, E., Neria, Y., Van Meter, P. E., Yihong, Z., Hembree, E., Lovell, K., Biyanova, T., & Marshall, R. D. (2015). Is exposure necessary? A randomized clinical trial of interpersonal psychotherapy for PTSD. *American Journal of Psychiatry, 172,* 430-440. doi:10.1176/appi.ajp.2014.14070908

Cusack, K., Jonas, D. E., Forneris, C. A., Wines, C., Sonis, J., Middleton, J. C., Feltner, C., Brownley, K. A., Olmsted, K. R., Greenblatt, A., & Gaynes, B. N. (2016). Psychological treatments for adults with posttraumatic stress disorder: A systematic review and meta-analysis. *Clinical Psychology Review, 43,* 128-141. doi:10.1016/j.cpr.2015.10.003

Alexander, P. C., Neimeyer, R. A., Follette, V. M., Moore, M. K., & Harter, S. L. (1989). A comparison of group treatments of women sexually abused as children. *Journal of Consulting and Clinical Psychology, 57,* 479-483. doi:10.1037//0022-006X.57.4.479

Chard, K. M. (2005). An evaluation of Cognitive Processing Therapy for the treatment of posttraumatic stress disorder related to childhood sexual abuse. *Journal of Consulting and Clinical Psychology, 75,* 965-971. doi:10.1037/0022-006X.73.5.965

Krupnik, J. L., Green, B. L., Stockton, P., Miranda, J., Krause, E. D., & Mete, M. (2008). Group interpersonal psychotherapy for low-income women with posttraumatic stress disorder. *Psychotherapy Research, 18,* 497-507. doi:10.1080/10503300802183678

Schnurr, P. P., Friedman, M. J., Foy, D. W., Shea, M. T., Hsieh, F. Y., & Lavori, P. W. (2003). Randomized trial of trauma-focused group therapy for posttraumatic stress disorder: Results from a Department of Veterans Affairs Cooperative Study. *Archives of General Psychiatry, 60,* 481-489. doi:10.1001/archpsyc.60.5.481

Zlotnick, C., Shea, M. T., Rosen, K. H., Simpson, E., Mulrenin, K., Begin, A., & Pearlstein, T. (1997). An affect-management group for women with posttraumatic stress disorder and histories of childhood sexual abuse. *Journal of Traumatic Stress, 10,* 425-436. doi:10.1002/jts.2490100308

Sloan, D. M., Feinstein, B. A., Gallagher, M. W., Beck, J. G., & Keane, T. M. (2013). Efficacy of group treatment for posttraumatic stress disorder symptoms: A meta-analysis. *Psychological Trauma: Theory, Research, Practice, and Policy, 5,* 176-183. doi:10.1037/a0026291

Linehan M. (1993). *Cognitive-behavioral treatment of borderline personality disorder.* New York: Guilford Press.

Cloitre, M., Stovall-McClough, K. C., Nooner, K., Zorbas, P., Cherry, S., Jackson, C. L. Gan, W., & Petkova, E. (2010). Treatment for PTSD related to childhood abuse: A randomized controlled trial. *American Journal of Psychiatry, 167,* 915-924. doi:10.1176/appi.ajp.22010.09081247

Walser, R. D., & Westrup, D. (2007). *Acceptance and Commitment Therapy for the treatment of post-traumatic stress disorder and trauma-related problems: A practitioner's guide to using mindfulness and acceptance strategies.* Oakland, CA: New Harbinger Publications.

Roberts, N. P., Roberts, P. A., Jones, N., & Bisson, J. I. (2015). Psychological interventions for post-traumatic stress disorder and comorbid substance use disorder: A systematic review and meta-analysis. *Clinical Psychology Review, 38,* 25-38. doi:10.1016/j.cpr.2015.02.007

Spiegel, H., & Spiegel, D. (2008). *Trance and treatment: Clinical uses of hypnosis.* Washington D.C.: American Psychiatric Association Publishing.

Brom, D., Kleber, R. J., & Defares, P. B. (1989). Brief psychotherapy for posttraumatic stress disorders. *Journal of Consulting and Clinical Psychology, 57,* 607-612. doi:10.1037/0022-006X.57.5.607

Foa, E. B., Rothbaum, B. O., Riggs, D. S., & Murdock, T. B. (1991). Treatment of posttraumatic stress disorder in rape victims: A comparison between cognitive-behavioral procedures and counseling. *Journal of Consulting and Clinical Psychology, 59,* 715-723. doi:10.1037/0022-006X.59.5.715

Monson, C. M., Fredman, S. J., Macdonald, A., Pukay-Martin, N. D., Resick, P. A., & Schnurr, P. P. (2102). Effect of cognitive-behavioral couple therapy for PTSD: A randomized controlled trial. *Journal of the American Medical Association, 308,* 700-709. doi:10.1001/jama.2012.9307

<u>A Letter to the Daughters of the King</u>

My beloved Daughter,

*You are not an object to be appreciated, a thing to be possessed, or a body to be coveted. You are so much more than the shell you reside in….**you are a soul, a spirit, a mind, and a heart….** You are my most prized creation, purposed and destined for great things only I can reveal to you; a child of a King, known by NAME….I not only know your name, but I know the number of the very hairs on your head. I know every thought, idea, desire, dream, and hope you have hidden deep inside. I created you in your mother's womb…there is nothing about you I do not know. No one can ever nor will ever know you the way I do. And with all of this knowledge, I love you with a relentless love that consumes every mistake you have made or may make. I will pursue you to the ends of the earth, until the end of your time, because that is how great my love for you is. When others criticize you, I look on you with adoration. When others walk away from you in distain, I reach for you with open arms. While others condemn you for your sins, I am so filled with love for you that I submit myself to the cross to die in your place. I LOVE YOU. Do you understand that?? Do you have any idea how much?? Neither life nor death nor angels or demons, nor the present nor the future, neither height nor depth, or anything else in all creation can separate you from MY*

LOVE. Nothing you can do can earn that love, and nothing you can do will stop my love. Stop letting others determine your value….find your value in ME. Your value, beloved, is BEYOND MEASURE.

Your loving Father,

ΎHẀH

YAHWEH

About the Author:

The author, Dr. Kristi Godwin, is a South Georgia native who began writing at age nine. She was first published at age 12, won several writing awards as a child, and published her first anthology at age 17. She is an avid reader who loves to learn and explore a variety of subjects, and earned degrees in Psychology, Marriage and Family Therapy, and Public Administration in her adulthood. She also is passionate about human rights and the ethical treatment of animals, and has been an activist in both areas throughout her life. She founded a non-profit organization in 2008 geared toward inner-city, at-risk youth, and worked as a licensed therapist with troubled children and youth for over a decade.

Dr. Godwin is also the mother of four children and resides with her children and pets in Georgia. She currently works as a therapist with women who have a history of trauma, and is active in ministry in her community. Works by Dr. Godwin include: A Collection of Poems, Words of Faith, White Anti-Racist Role Models, The Second Industrial Revolution Is Upon Us: The Future of Managing Human Resources in Public Administration (an anthology), Memoirs of a Southern Girl: The Story of My Life, Yea, Though I Walk…, Healing Beyond Trauma, and A New Season of Poetry.

Find Dr. Godwin on Amazon and follow her Author Page to be notified of her new publications. For personal inquiries on how to address your own trauma or abuse history you may email her at: drkristibgodwin.author@yahoo.com.

Author Blog Page: www.BeTheAuthorOfYourLifeBook.blogspot.com

Author Facebook Page: www.facebook.com/BeTheAuthorOfYourLifeBook/

89624069R00091

Made in the USA
Middletown, DE
18 September 2018